ChatGPT Prompt Engineering With Tech Trends

A Comprehensive Guide to Emerging Technologies

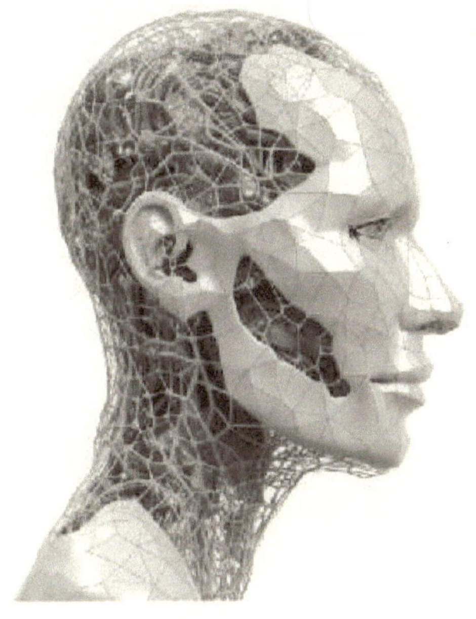

ATHEER MAHIR

First Edition

11 April 2023

ChatGPT Prompt Engineering With Tech Trends -A Comprehensive Guide to Emerging Technologies

by Atheer Mahir

April 2023:   First Edition

Revision History for the first Edition

2023-04-11 First Release

Contents:

Introduction

Welcome to Tech Trends! In an ever-evolving world of technology, it can be challenging to keep up with the latest breakthroughs, products, and tools that shape our digital landscape. As we venture into this exciting era of innovation, you might be asking yourself:

- What are these new tools and technologies?

- Why are they potentially important?

- If there are controversies, what's being said on each side?

- And as a technologist, what do you need to do to learn more and prepare for how they may affect the way you work?

My name is Atheer Mahir, and I am thrilled to present this comprehensive guide to the most promising and transformative technologies that are currently emerging in the industry. Tech Trends aims to address these pressing questions and provide you with a clear understanding of the most important emerging technologies, their potential impact, and how they might affect your professional and personal life.

In this book, you will find valuable insights into cutting-edge products and tools, along with detailed analyses of the debates and controversies that surround them. My objective is to equip you with the knowledge and resources necessary to stay ahead of the curve and capitalise on the opportunities that these new technologies present.

Join me on this enlightening journey as we explore the fascinating world of tech trends and unlock the secrets of the technologies that are shaping our future. Together, let's embrace the endless possibilities and challenges that lie ahead, and prepare ourselves for a brighter and more connected tomorrow.

1. Emerging Technologies: The Very Latest

1.1 AI-Assisted Programming

As we step into the future of software development, AI-assisted programming has become a game-changer. Chances are, you have already come across conversations or demonstrations about using tools like ChatGPT for programming. By providing a simple prompt, AI generates fully written code that can be easily integrated into your project. In this sub-chapter, we will discuss the concept of AI as a programming partner, its capabilities, inner workings, and what to expect in the near future.

There are numerous AI-assisted programming tools available, but we will focus on three key players: ChatGPT, Microsoft Bing, and GitHub Copilot. These tools offer a solid framework for understanding the technology and represent the variety of tools on the market.

AI-assisted programming tools are generative in nature, meaning they can create code based on prompts. Beyond code generation, they can also detect errors, explain code functionality, add comments, reformat code, translate languages, and even write tests. Specialised tools like GitHub Copilot can even anticipate your thoughts, acting as a highly intelligent auto-complete feature.

These AI tools enable developers to write code more efficiently and quickly, saving time by offering ready-to-use examples, patterns, and prototypes. The secret behind AI's ability to write code lies in the fact that code is just another form of language. Large language models like ChatGPT are trained using coding languages, allowing them to generate code-like sentences based on their training data.

However, it's crucial to understand that there is no conscious, intelligent agent within these systems actively writing code. Instead, generative AI interprets prompts and constructs sentences by statistically guessing the next word. Because coding languages are more structured and patterned than human languages, AI-generated code is often functional.

AI programming tools have different approaches and strengths. ChatGPT is a general-purpose model that can interact with data, while Bing uses ChatGPT as an interface between users and the internet. On the other hand, GitHub Copilot is a specialised AI programming tool embedded within code editors.

1.1.1 ChatGPT

ChatGPT, developed by OpenAI, is a generative pre-trained transformer language model. It has received attention for its ability to generate human-like text based on provided prompts. While it's mainly designed to interact with data, it can also generate code-like sentences

when given the right input. However, it's limited by the knowledge in its training data, which was last updated in September 2021. To learn more about ChatGPT, visit the OpenAI website:

- OpenAI's ChatGPT: https://platform.openai.com/docs/guides/chat

1.1.2 Microsoft Bing

Microsoft Bing is a search engine that integrates AI-powered features like ChatGPT to provide an improved user experience. When given a prompt, Bing searches the internet for relevant information and then generates responses that include links to authoritative sources. This allows users to verify the information provided and explore further if needed. To learn more about Microsoft Bing and its AI capabilities, visit the following resources:

- Microsoft Bing: https://www.bing.com/

- Microsoft AI: https://www.microsoft.com/en-us/ai

1.1.3 GitHub Copilot

GitHub Copilot is a specialised AI-assisted programming tool developed by GitHub and OpenAI. It works as an AI-powered code completion tool, providing developers with code suggestions based on their input. Copilot is designed to adapt to a developer's coding style and can generate code for various programming languages and frameworks. The official GitHub Copilot website offers more information and a preview of its features:

- GitHub Copilot: https://copilot.github.com/

By leveraging these AI tools, developers can write code more efficiently and quickly. They save time by offering ready-to-use examples, patterns, and prototypes. AI's ability to write code lies in the fact that code is just another form of language. Large language models like ChatGPT are trained using coding languages, allowing them to generate code-like sentences based on their training data.

To make the most of AI-assisted programming tools, it is essential to:

1. Integrate them into your workflow.

2. Source information from reliable AI tools.

3. Maintain a solid understanding of modern coding standards and best practices.

To stay updated with the latest advancements in AI-assisted programming, consider following the official blogs and news sections of OpenAI, Microsoft, and GitHub:

- OpenAI Blog: https://openai.com/blog/

- Microsoft AI Blog: https://blogs.microsoft.com/ai/

- GitHub Blog: https://github.blog/

By exploring these resources and integrating AI-assisted programming into your work, you will be better equipped to navigate the ever-evolving landscape of software development.

In conclusion, AI programming tools are valuable resources for developers and are continually improving. While they are not yet advanced enough to replace human programmers, they save significant time in code writing and research. To make the most of these tools, it is essential to integrate them into your workflow, source information from reliable AI tools, and maintain a solid understanding of modern coding standards and best practices. Embrace AI-assisted programming today and enhance your coding experience.

1.2 Generative Pre-trained Transformers (GPT-4)

1.2.1 Introduction to GPT-4

Generative Pre-trained Transformers (GPT) are a series of increasingly powerful AI language models developed by OpenAI. The most recent release, GPT-4, is a significant advancement in the GPT series, offering improved reasoning, concise answers, and several new capabilities. In this section, we will explore the differences between GPT-3 and GPT-4, the new features introduced in GPT-4, and its applications in various industries.

1.2.2 Understanding GPT

GPT stands for Generative Pre-trained Transformer. It is a neural network that generates content, such as stories or art, using massive amounts of data. As a transformer, it identifies keywords from human input and infers intent to provide contextually relevant responses. However, without specific details, it makes assumptions based on the most likely correct answer for a given situation.

1.2.3 GPT-3 vs. GPT-4

GPT-4 is a significant improvement over its predecessor, GPT-3. While GPT-4 is slower and requires more computational power, it offers better reasoning and more concise answers. OpenAI has fine-tuned GPT-4 to reduce hallucinations, biases, and improve overall safety.

GPT-4 is integrated into OpenAI's ChatGPT Plus subscription, Microsoft's Bing, Microsoft 365, and Azure. Its performance on tasks such as passing the bar exam, a test for lawyers, has improved significantly, moving from the lower 10th percentile in GPT-3 to the top 10th percentile in GPT-4.

1.2.4 GPT-4's Enhanced Capabilities

GPT-4 has several new features that set it apart from its predecessor:

- Expanded input size: GPT-4 can accept up to 25,000 words of text, enabling it to process longer inputs and provide more detailed outputs.

- Improved steerability: Users can control GPT-4's personality, verbosity, and style more effectively. For instance, they can request a Socratic mode where GPT-4 guides users to answers through leading questions.

- Image and graphic understanding: GPT-4 can interpret photos and graphics, opening up possibilities for new applications, such as providing recipes based on fridge contents or interpreting data from charts and graphs.

1.2.5 Applications and Integrations

GPT-4 is being integrated into various aspects of everyday life, with ChatGPT becoming the fastest-growing product in technology history. GitHub Copilot, powered by GPT-4, has helped developers become 88% more productive. Companies like Duolingo, Stripe, and Morgan Stanley have implemented GPT-4 into their products.

Microsoft's recently announced Semantic Kernel is an open-source SDK that simplifies GPT-4 and other AI integrations into applications. GPT-4's features will also be integrated into Microsoft 365 apps, including Excel, Word, and PowerPoint, enhancing productivity.

1.2.6 The Future of GPT-4

GPT-4 represents a significant upgrade in AI language models, changing how we interact with the digital world. As developers continue to integrate GPT-4's capabilities into applications, users can expect new features, image inputs, enhanced accuracy, and a higher level of creativity. The future of GPT-4 is filled with possibilities, and it is poised to revolutionise numerous industries and applications.

1.2.7 Useful resources and references

1. OpenAI's introduction to ChatGPT: https://platform.openai.com/docs/guides/chatgpt

2. OpenAI's blog post on GPT-3: https://openai.com/blog/openai-api/

3. A detailed paper on GPT-3: https://arxiv.org/abs/2005.14165

4. OpenAI's ChatGPT Plus subscription: https://openai.com/chatgpt-pricing/

5. Microsoft's Bing: https://www.bing.com/

6. Microsoft 365: https://www.microsoft.com/en/microsoft-365

7. Azure AI: https://azure.microsoft.com/en-us/services/cognitive-services/

8. GitHub Copilot: https://copilot.github.com/

9. Duolingo: https://www.duolingo.com/

10. Stripe: https://stripe.com/

11. Morgan Stanley: https://www.morganstanley.com/

GPT-4 offers significant improvements over its predecessor, GPT-3, including better reasoning, more concise answers, and the ability to process longer inputs. It also provides improved steerability and can interpret photos and graphics. GPT-4 has been integrated into various applications and industries, enhancing productivity and revolutionising user experiences. The future of GPT-4 is filled with possibilities, as it continues to impact the way we interact with digital technology.

1.3 AI-driven Development Environments

Imagine a world where developers no longer spend countless hours poring over lines of code. Instead, they have a powerful AI assistant to streamline their work and enhance their productivity. This futuristic vision is now a reality, thanks to GitHub Copilot.

GitHub Copilot, released in June 2022, has undergone significant improvements since its inception, including a version tailored for businesses. This AI-driven development environment has made a notable impact on the way developers work and has transformed the landscape of software development.

GitHub's research and usage data revealed that Copilot generated 46% of developers' code across all programming languages and 61% for Java developers. Additionally, 90% of developers reported completing tasks faster with Copilot, and 75% experienced a better ability to focus on more satisfying work.

These impressive results highlight the effectiveness of Copilot, which is powered by an improved OpenAI Codex model. The newer model, known as Fill In the Middle (FIM), analyzes code both before and after the insertion point to offer more contextual suggestions. This enhanced understanding helps developers write more efficient and accurate code.

Furthermore, GitHub has introduced a lightweight client-side model that monitors user preferences and behavior. By tracking accepted suggestions, Copilot can provide more precise and personalized recommendations. This AI-assistant also excels in preventing the suggestion of insecure code to users.

With the release of Copilot for Business, enterprise features such as license and policy management, proxy support, and corporate VPN compatibility have been introduced. Priced at $19 per seat, the business plan offers companies the ability to utilize Copilot without storing their code on GitHub. Moreover, developers can integrate their code with other editors like JetBrains Visual Studio and Neovim.

As AI-driven development environments like Copilot for Business continue to evolve, they are revolutionizing the efficiency and quality of software development across various industries. Embrace the future of coding and experience a new level of creativity and productivity with Copilot.

Useful resources:

1. GitHub Copilot - Official Website: https://copilot.github.com/

2. GitHub Copilot - Official Documentation: https://docs.github.com/en/codespaces/github-copilot

3. OpenAI Codex - Official Website: https://openai.com/research/codex/

4. OpenAI Codex - Official Documentation: https://platform.openai.com/docs/guides/codex

5. GitHub Copilot: Your AI pair programmer - Official Blog Post: https://github.blog/2021-06-29-introducing-github-copilot-ai-pair-programmer/

6. GitHub Copilot for Business - Pricing: https://github.com/pricing

1.4 ChatGPT

Imagine attending a lively party, full of engaging conversations and thought-provoking exchanges. Now imagine a machine taking part in those discussions, offering insights and answering questions with the same level of nuance as its human counterparts. That's the reality we're approaching with ChatGPT, an AI-powered conversational tool that's revolutionising the way we interact with technology.

ChatGPT, an online application that launched in November 2022, quickly gained popularity, reaching one million users in just five days. Powered by a set of technologies called Generative Pre-trained Transformers (GPT), ChatGPT aims to create new content by leveraging up to 175 billion parameters. It utilises a transformer architecture, enabling it to excel at understanding and processing human language.

Developed by OpenAI, a company with a mission to create Artificial General Intelligences (AGIs) that can perform any intellectual task a human can do, ChatGPT is part of a broader effort to develop AI systems that benefit humanity rather than replace it. OpenAI is also behind other groundbreaking products like DALL·E 2, an AI system for generating realistic art, and Whisper, a speech recognition, translation, and transcription system that approaches human-like synthetic speech.

The secret behind ChatGPT's human-like performance lies in the models and algorithms developers have created to mimic human problem-solving processes. By using autoregressive models, ChatGPT can predict results based on past values, giving the impression that it understands not only what users ask but also what they likely mean.

Beyond conversations, ChatGPT is capable of writing essays, scripts, resumes, and songs, as well as performing more complex tasks like writing and debugging code. However, it does have limitations, such as providing incorrect answers authoritatively and having limited knowledge of current events due to its training data being based mostly on information up to 2021.

Despite its shortcomings, ChatGPT holds immense potential for speeding up the development of tasks and helping humans iterate on ideas. With APIs available for developers and entrepreneurs, the technology can be integrated into new and innovative products. Ultimately, professionals who understand how to work with AI tools like ChatGPT will have a significant advantage in the evolving digital landscape.

Here are some resources you can use as references in your book for the sub-chapter "1.4 ChatGPT":

1. ChatGPT - Official Website: https://www.openai.com/chatgpt/

2. OpenAI - Official Website: https://openai.com/

3. OpenAI's DALL·E 2: https://www.openai.com/dall-e-2/

4. OpenAI's Whisper: https://openai.com/research/whisper

5. OpenAI's Codex (which is the foundation for ChatGPT): https://openai.com/blog/openai-codex

6. OpenAI's GPT-3: https://openai.com/blog/gpt-3-apps

1.5 Ethereum merge

Picture a world where the technology that powers our digital transactions evolves, becoming more efficient and environmentally friendly. That's the vision that came to life when Ethereum, one of the largest blockchains and cryptocurrencies, underwent the Ethereum Merge in September 2022. This major technological shift changed the blockchain's underlying consensus model from Proof of Work to Proof of Stake.

To better understand the Ethereum Merge's significance, let's delve into the basics of blockchain technology. Blockchains are decentralised, trustless systems where transactions are stored in immutable containers called blocks. These blocks are locked and added to the chain, ensuring their contents remain unaltered.

Decentralisation means that instead of relying on a central authority like a bank, everyone on the network has a copy of the ledger, making transactions more secure and transparent.

However, decentralisation also introduces the double spend problem, where someone could potentially spend the same coins twice by taking advantage of delays in the system. To overcome this issue, cryptocurrencies use consensus mechanisms, incentivizing network users to validate legitimate transactions and add them to blocks in exchange for coins.

Before the Ethereum Merge, both Bitcoin and Ethereum used the Proof of Work model, which requires validators (miners) to perform energy-intensive computations to add new blocks to the blockchain. This model has been criticised for its environmental impact.

The Ethereum Merge transitioned Ethereum to the Proof of Stake model, where validators "stake" their cryptocurrency, essentially putting it in escrow, to prove their trustworthiness. Validators who approve invalid blocks or scam transactions risk losing their staked coins. The Merge promises to reduce Ethereum's energy footprint by up to 99% compared to the Proof of Work model, making it a more sustainable choice.

It's essential to note that the Ethereum Merge is a technological change, addressing energy consumption but not necessarily solving all other underlying issues with cryptocurrencies.

Here are some resources you can use as references in your book for the sub-chapter "1.5 Ethereum Merge":

1. Ethereum - Official Website: https://ethereum.org/

2. Ethereum Improvement Proposals (EIPs): https://eips.ethereum.org/

3. Ethereum Foundation Blog: https://blog.ethereum.org/

1.6 Prompt Engineering[1]

As AI systems become increasingly sophisticated, prompt engineering emerges as an essential discipline to ensure effective communication and interaction with AI models. In this context, prompt engineering comprises several crucial aspects.

1. Prompt Design Principles: The foundation of prompt engineering lies in crafting clear and concise prompts. Effective prompts convey specific goals, minimise ambiguity, and set the right context for the AI system. Designing appropriate prompts involves understanding the AI model's limitations and strengths, ensuring the model produces the desired output.

---

[1] Appendix A - Advanced Prompt Engineering

2. Prompt Variations and A/B Testing: Creating multiple variations of prompts helps determine the most effective prompt for a specific task. A/B testing allows for the comparison of different prompts, measuring their performance and identifying the best option for a given use-case.

   A/B testing, also known as split testing or bucket testing, is a method of comparing two versions of a variable, in this case, prompts, to determine which one performs better. This testing technique is commonly used in marketing, web design, and product development to optimise user experience, conversion rates, and overall performance.

   In the context of prompt engineering, A/B testing involves creating two or more variations of a prompt and presenting them to different subsets of users or AI systems. The performance of each prompt variation is measured based on predefined evaluation criteria, such as the quality of the AI system's response, user engagement, or task completion rate. By comparing the results, prompt engineers can identify the most effective prompt for a specific task and refine the communication with the AI system accordingly.

   A/B testing helps ensure that the AI system understands the user's intent more accurately and generates more relevant, useful, and coherent outputs, ultimately improving the overall user experience.

3. Personalisation and Context-Awareness: As AI systems become more advanced, prompts can be tailored to individual users and contexts. This personalisation enhances the user experience and improves the AI system's understanding of user preferences, goals, and requirements.

4. Prompt Repository and Management: Managing prompts at scale requires organising and storing them efficiently. A well-structured

prompt repository allows for easy access, modification, and reuse of prompts, streamlining the prompt engineering process.

5. Evaluation Metrics and Quality Control: Establishing evaluation metrics helps assess the performance of prompts and the AI system's responses. These metrics can include accuracy, fluency, relevance, and coherence. Continuous monitoring and improvement ensure the AI system's outputs meet the desired quality standards.

6. Ethical Considerations: Prompt engineering must take into account ethical concerns, such as avoiding biases, ensuring data privacy, and preventing AI systems from generating harmful or inappropriate content.

The growth of prompt engineering as a discipline signifies the increasing importance of AI-human interaction and the necessity for effective communication with AI systems. By focusing on the design, management, and optimisation of prompts, prompt engineering can significantly improve the AI user experience across various industries and applications.

For further reading and research, consider exploring these resources:

1. "Prompt design" by OpenAI https://platform.openai.com/docs/guides/completion/prompt-design.

2. "Better language models and their implications" by OpenAI https://openai.com/research/better-language-models.

3. "AI and compute" by OpenAI https://openai.com/research/ai-and-compute.

These resources should provide valuable information and guidance for your sub-chapter on prompt engineering.

2. Artificial Intelligence

2.1 Generative AI Models

Generative AI models are a subset of artificial intelligence that focuses on creating new patterns or outputs based on the data it has been trained on. These models can be applied to a wide range of tasks, such as generating images, composing music, and even writing code. In this chapter, we will discuss how generative AI models work, their applications, and their limitations.

One of the key aspects of generative AI models is their ability to recognise patterns. For example, when you look at a series of images related to Halloween, your brain can easily predict the next image in the sequence. Similarly, generative AI models can be trained to recognise patterns in data and use that information to create new patterns or outputs.

Generative AI models can be applied to various tasks, such as:

1. Image generation: By training an AI model on a dataset of images, such as faces or objects, the model can learn the

patterns and generate new, realistic images. A popular example of this application is the website thispersondoesnotexist.com, which generates random human faces using a generative AI model.

2. Music composition: AI models can be trained on different music genres, learning the patterns and structures of various styles. These models can then generate original music compositions based on the patterns they have learned. Musi-co is an example of a platform that utilises AI for music composition.

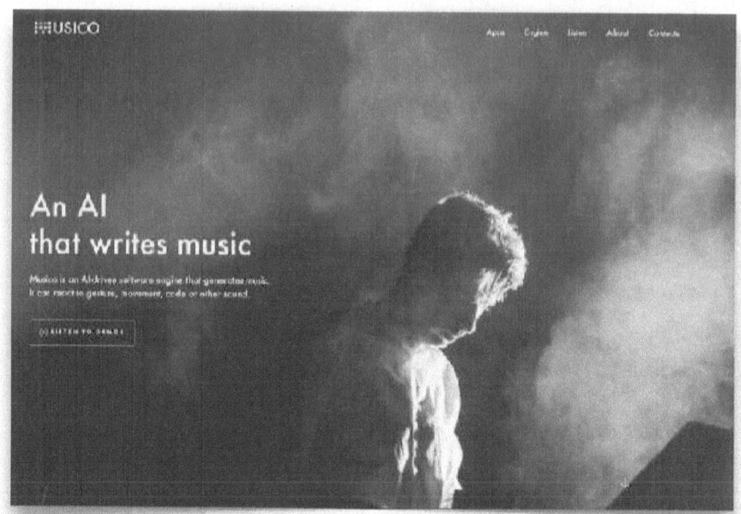

3. Deepfakes: Generative AI models can be used to create realistic fake videos by replacing faces in existing footage. Websites like

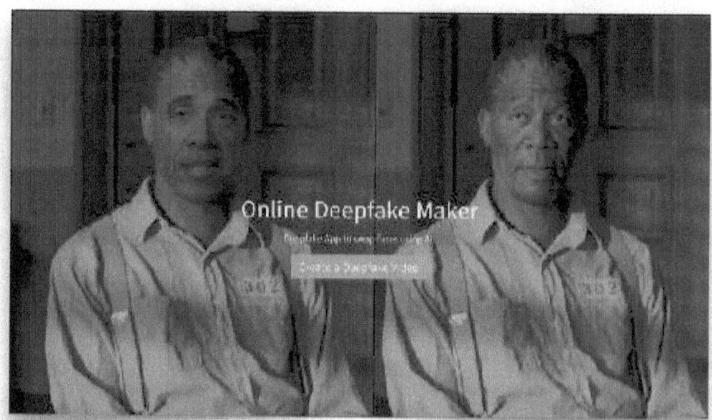

deepfakesweb.com provide tools and services for creating deepfake videos.

4. Text generation: AI models like GPT-3 have been trained on billions of parameters, enabling them to generate human-like text. Tools like Compose AI utilise this technology to create content, while other applications like GitHub's Copilot help

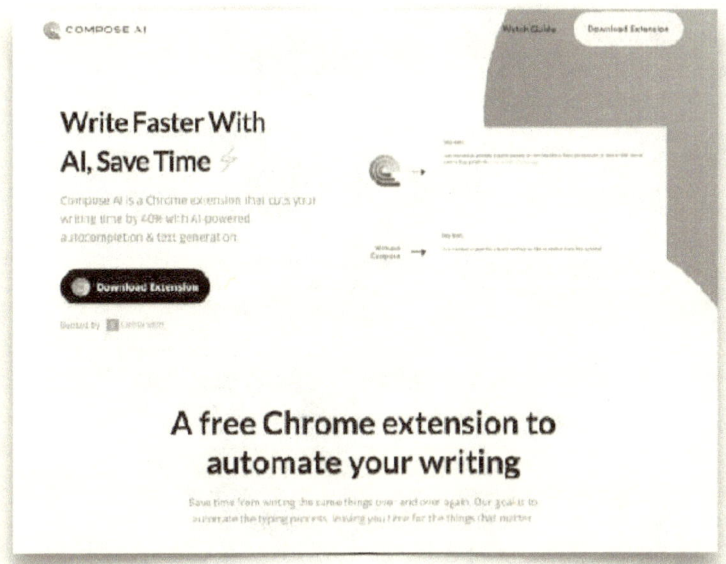

programmers write entire functions and reduce code generation time.

Despite the impressive capabilities of generative AI models, there are several limitations:

1. Data requirements: Generative AI models require massive amounts of data to generate high-quality results. The more data the model has been trained on, the better its outputs will be.

2. Unpredictable results: Generative AI models may not always generate the desired output. For example, with code generation tools like Copilot, users cannot always trust that the generated code will work as intended.

3. Lack of novelty: Generative AI models can only create outputs based on the patterns they have already learned. They are not capable of generating entirely new concepts or ideas.

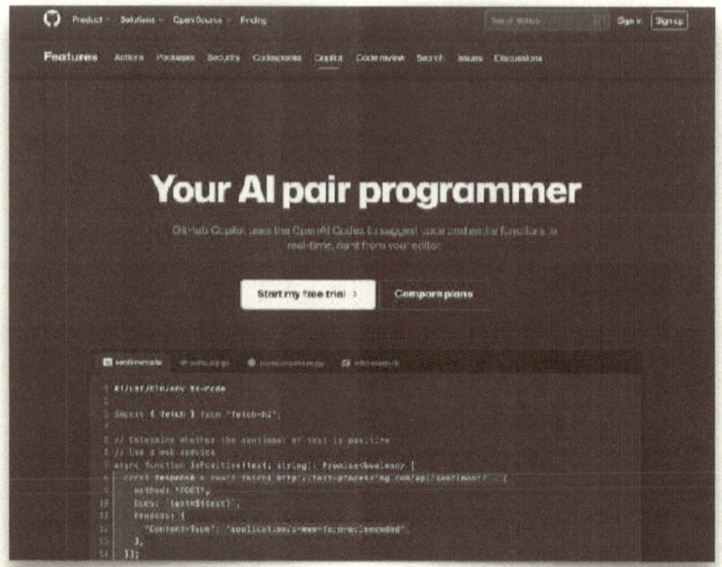

In conclusion, generative AI models are a powerful and emerging technology with a wide range of applications. Although they have some limitations, they excel at processing large datasets, generating numerous options, and reducing the time it takes to complete repetitive tasks. As these models continue to develop, they have the potential to revolutionise various industries and the way we interact with technology.

Websites:

https://this-person-does-not-exist.com/en

https://musi-co.com/

https://deepfakesweb.com/

https://www.compose.ai/

https://github.com/features/copilot/

2.2 AI-powered Code Assistants

AI-powered code assistants, such as GitHub Copilot, are revolutionising the way programmers write code by leveraging the power of artificial intelligence. These advanced tools generate entire functions, predict coding patterns, and improve overall coding efficiency, making them an indispensable part of the software development process. In this sub-chapter, we will explore the technology behind AI-powered code assistants, discuss their current capabilities and limitations, and examine their potential impact on the software development industry.

2.2.1 GitHub Copilot: A Revolutionary AI-driven Tool

GitHub Copilot is an AI-driven code assistant designed to write entire functions for programmers in various languages, based on the context of their code. It utilises a technology called GPT-3 (Generative Pre-trained Transformer), a natural language processor capable of predicting text based on extensive data. This allows GPT-3 to perform tasks such as answering questions or generating sentences.

The underlying algorithm of GitHub Copilot, called Codex, is specifically tailored to focus on software source code. Codex is highly compatible with popular programming languages and frameworks, especially those with vast amounts of publicly available code, such as Python, JavaScript, and Ruby. Microsoft, the owner of GitHub, has invested $1 billion in OpenAI, the company responsible for developing Codex.

GitHub Copilot synthesises code from various public sources, such as existing GitHub repositories. As more users utilise the tool, Codex continues to learn, providing increasingly accurate and efficient solutions. To activate Copilot, programmers can begin writing a function with a meaningful name, and the tool will attempt to generate the entire function. Alternatively, a detailed comment can be provided to query the Codex.

The code generated by Copilot is not simply copied from open-source repositories but is instead brand new code produced by the algorithm. The tool's accuracy is impressive, positioning it as the next generation of auto-complete functionality for coding.

2.2.2 Current Capabilities and Limitations

While AI-powered code assistants like GitHub Copilot offer significant advantages, they also have certain limitations. The accuracy and usefulness of the generated code are directly related to the quality and quantity of the training data. This means that for less popular languages or niche programming scenarios, the performance of the AI may be less reliable.

Moreover, AI-generated code may not always adhere to best practices or specific coding standards. Developers still need to review and optimise the generated code to ensure it meets the requirements of their projects. In some cases, the AI may produce code that is not entirely functional or requires further refinement.

Another limitation is the potential for AI-generated code to introduce security vulnerabilities or other unintended consequences. As with any tool, it is crucial for developers to carefully review and test the generated code before integrating it into their projects.

2.2.3 The Future of AI-powered Code Assistants

Despite their current limitations, AI-powered code assistants like GitHub Copilot have immense potential to transform the software development process. As these tools continue to evolve, they will likely become even more accurate and efficient, making them indispensable for programmers.

In the future, AI-powered code assistants may not only generate code but also provide real-time assistance with debugging, code optimisation, and refactoring. This would allow developers to focus on higher-level tasks, such as designing software architecture or implementing complex algorithms, while the AI takes care of routine coding tasks.

Furthermore, as AI technology advances, it is expected that these tools will be able to understand and generate code for a wider range of programming languages and frameworks, making them even more versatile and valuable for developers.

The growing adoption of AI-powered code assistants will also drive the need for new training methods and evaluation metrics. Developers and researchers will need to collaborate to create more sophisticated models that can learn from an ever-expanding range of sources, including code repositories, technical documentation, and even human interactions.

In conclusion,AI-powered code assistants, like GitHub Copilot, have the potential to reshape the software development landscape significantly. By automating routine coding tasks and providing real-time assistance, these tools enable developers to focus on more complex and creative aspects of their work. As AI technology continues to advance, we can expect further improvements in the accuracy, efficiency, and versatility of AI-driven code assistants, making them invaluable tools for developers across various programming languages and domains.

In addition, the integration of AI-powered code assistants into popular development environments and platforms will streamline the development process, resulting in faster and more efficient software creation. As more organisations and developers adopt these tools, we can expect to see a shift in the skillset required for software development, with a greater emphasis on high-level problem-solving, architecture design, and collaboration.

However, the increased reliance on AI-powered code assistants also highlights the need for ethical considerations and potential challenges. Developers and organisations must address concerns related to the potential misuse of AI-generated code, security vulnerabilities, and the impact of AI-driven automation on the job market.

By understanding and addressing these challenges, the software development community can harness the full potential of AI-powered code assistants to revolutionise the way software is created, maintained, and evolved, ultimately leading to a more efficient and innovative software development ecosystem.

Resources:

https://github.com/features/copilot/

https://openai.com/blog/openai-codex

https://github.com/OpenMindClub/awesome-chatgpt

https://www.cnbc.com/2023/04/08/microsofts-complex-bet-on-openai-brings-potential-and-uncertainty.html

2.3 AI in Biometrics and Facial Recognition

A few years ago, the FBI successfully apprehended a fugitive after a decade-long manhunt, thanks to facial recognition technology. The fugitive had assumed a false identity and was living under the radar. However, when he applied for a passport using his new identity, the facial recognition system matched his photo to an older one in the database, alerting the authorities and leading to his arrest. This real-life story highlights the power and potential implications of facial recognition technology, which relies on advanced algorithms, high-speed internet, cloud services, high-resolution cameras, and artificial intelligence (AI) to identify individuals from photos or videos.

Facial recognition starts with data collection. For years, facial recognition companies have gathered publicly available photos and videos, using them to train algorithms to detect faces and recognize distinct facial features. These models enable the identification of individuals from images and videos. As facial recognition technology becomes increasingly ubiquitous, it is being integrated into various aspects of daily life, from unlocking devices to monitoring students and aiding law enforcement efforts.

There are both positive and negative implications of facial recognition technology. On one hand, it simplifies many routine tasks, such as unlocking devices, verifying identities, and providing valuable tools for crime prevention and investigation. For instance, it can be used to locate missing persons, identify suspects in criminal investigations, and even prevent identity fraud.

On the other hand, facial recognition technology raises significant ethical concerns related to privacy, surveillance, and potential biases. One major issue is that the machine learning models underpinning facial recognition technology are only as accurate as the data they are trained on. Numerous studies have exposed racial and other biases in facial recognition systems, sometimes leading to detrimental consequences for underrepresented groups. For example, in 2018, the American Civil Liberties Union (ACLU) revealed that Amazon's facial recognition software incorrectly matched 28 members of the US Congress to criminal mugshots, with a disproportionate number of false matches involving people of colour.

Additionally, facial recognition impacts privacy, as the images and videos used to train the algorithms are often collected without individuals' consent or knowledge. Once a person's face is in the system, removing it is nearly impossible. This raises concerns about mass surveillance, as facial recognition technology can be used to track individuals without their knowledge, potentially leading to a loss of personal privacy and autonomy.

As facial recognition technology continues to evolve and improve, it is essential for consumers to educate themselves about the technology

and the potential risks associated with it. Developers working with facial recognition should prioritise privacy by design and informed consent, while also addressing the issue of AI and machine learning bias. They should actively work on refining algorithms to minimise bias and improve accuracy, ensuring that the technology is as fair and equitable as possible.

Companies, organisations, and government agencies looking to implement facial recognition technology should deploy it responsibly, obtaining informed consent, exercising due diligence in vendor selection, and limiting the scope of facial recognition to situations where it is absolutely necessary. They should also consider the ethical implications of the technology, especially when dealing with sensitive data or vulnerable populations.

Moreover, governments should establish comprehensive regulatory frameworks to govern the use of facial recognition technology. This includes creating guidelines for data collection, storage, and usage, as well as defining the rights and responsibilities of different stakeholders involved in the technology's development and deployment. Legislation should also address the potential misuse of facial recognition technology by both public and private entities, ensuring that the technology is used in a manner that respects individual rights and upholds democratic values.

In conclusion, although facial recognition technology offers convenience and potential benefits in various applications, it is crucial to carefully consider the impact on privacy, security, and civil liberties. The question remains: Is the cost of facial recognition to our privacy and security a price we are willing to pay? This discussion warrants ongoing dialogue and collaboration among stakeholders, including developers, policymakers, and the public, to ensure that the technology is used ethically and responsibly.

To delve deeper into the various aspects of facial recognition technology, we can break down the topic into several sub-sections:

The development of facial recognition technology can be traced back to the 1960s when Woody Bledsoe, Helen Chan Wolf, and Charles Bisson worked on a semi-automated system for recognizing human faces. This early effort laid the groundwork for subsequent advancements in the field. In the 1970s, Goldstein, Harmon, and Lesk introduced the first topographical approach to facial recognition, focusing on facial features such as eyes, nose, and mouth.

A significant milestone in the development of facial recognition technology came in the 1980s with the introduction of the Eigenface method by Sirovich and Kirby. The Eigenface technique used linear algebra to analyse and represent human faces, drastically improving the efficiency and accuracy of facial recognition algorithms.

In the 1990s and early 2000s, the development of advanced algorithms, such as Elastic Bunch Graph Matching (EBGM) and Fisherface, further improved the performance of facial recognition systems. The availability of larger datasets and increased computing power allowed for more sophisticated techniques to be employed.

With the advent of deep learning and convolutional neural networks (CNNs) in the 2010s, facial recognition technology experienced a significant leap in accuracy and performance. Deep learning enabled algorithms to learn and recognise complex patterns in facial images, even under varying lighting conditions, poses, and expressions.

2.3.2 Applications of Facial Recognition Technology

Facial recognition technology has found numerous applications across various domains:

- Personal device security: Many smartphones, laptops, and other personal devices now use facial recognition as a secure and convenient method for user authentication.

- Public safety: Surveillance systems in public spaces, such as airports, train stations, and malls, use facial recognition to identify potential security threats and locate missing persons.

- Border control: Immigration and customs authorities use facial recognition to verify the identity of travellers, streamlining the border-crossing process.

- Marketing: Retailers employ facial recognition to analyse customer demographics, preferences, and behaviour, allowing for targeted advertising and personalised shopping experiences.

- Healthcare: Facial recognition technology is used for patient identification, remote monitoring, and diagnosis of certain conditions, such as facial paralysis or genetic disorders.

- Education: Schools and universities use facial recognition for attendance tracking, access control, and ensuring student safety.

2.3.3 Ethical Concerns and Challenges

The use of facial recognition technology raises several ethical concerns and challenges:

- Privacy: The widespread use of facial recognition technology infringes on individual privacy, as people can be tracked and identified without their knowledge or consent.

- Surveillance: The technology can be employed for mass surveillance by governments, potentially leading to the suppression of dissent and violation of civil liberties.

- Biases: Facial recognition algorithms have been found to exhibit biases, with higher error rates for people of colour, women, and other underrepresented groups.

- False positives and negatives: Incorrect identifications by facial recognition systems can lead to unjust consequences, such as false arrests or denial of services.

2.3.4 Regulatory Landscape and Future Trends

Governments worldwide are grappling with the regulation of facial recognition technology to balance the benefits and risks associated with its use. The European Union's General Data Protection Regulation (GDPR) provides guidelines for the ethical use of facial recognition, requiring user consent and transparency. The California Privacy Rights

Act (CPRA) in the United States also imposes strict rules on the use of facial recognition technology.

Future trends in facial recognition technology include ongoing advancements in AI and machine learning, which will further improve the accuracy and efficiency of recognition systems. New applications and integration with other technologies, such as augmented reality and the Internet of Things, are also expected. However, the ethical debate surrounding facial recognition technology will likely continue, with growing calls for stricter regulation, greater transparency, and public accountability.

As facial recognition technology advances, efforts to address its ethical concerns are also expected to evolve. Research into "fairness-aware" algorithms aims to reduce biases in facial recognition systems, and privacy-enhancing techniques such as differential privacy and federated learning may help alleviate privacy concerns.

In the regulatory landscape, countries may adopt a more nuanced approach to the use of facial recognition technology, with varying levels of restriction based on the specific application and context. For example, law enforcement use might require a higher threshold for justification and oversight compared to personal device security.

The development of international standards and best practices for facial recognition technology will be crucial in ensuring its responsible and ethical deployment. Collaboration between governments, industry stakeholders, and civil society organisations will be essential to address the complex ethical, legal, and social implications of this rapidly evolving technology.

In conclusion, facial recognition technology holds immense potential for improving security, convenience, and efficiency across various domains. However, its widespread adoption also raises significant ethical concerns and challenges. By understanding the historical development of facial recognition technology, its diverse applications, the ethical issues it presents, and the regulatory landscape, we can better navigate the future of this powerful technology while ensuring that its benefits are realised without compromising individual privacy, civil liberties, and social equity.

3. Web3 and Related Technologies

3.1 Decentralised Internet (Web3)

3.1.1 A Brief History of the Internet: From Web 1.0 to Web 2.0

To understand the concept of Web3, or the decentralised internet, it's essential to recognise the evolution of the internet from its inception. Web 1.0, the first iteration of the internet, was a relatively static platform primarily consisting of HTML pages with limited interactivity. During this era, users were mainly passive consumers of content, with communication flowing one-way from organisations and content creators to the audience.

Web 2.0 marked a significant shift in the internet landscape, fostering greater interactivity and user-generated content. This era was characterised by the rise of social media, blogs, and other platforms that enabled users to create, share, and collaborate on content. However, despite its seemingly democratic nature, Web 2.0 became increasingly

centralised, with a few dominant platforms controlling vast amounts of user data and dictating the flow of information.

3.1.2 Introduction to Web3: Decentralised, Open, and Trustless

Web3 represents a new paradigm in the evolution of the internet, aiming to return power and control to individual users while addressing the shortcomings of centralised Web 2.0 platforms. Although there is no definitive definition of Web3, the concept generally revolves around several key principles:

- Decentralisation: Web3 seeks to eliminate centralised intermediaries by leveraging blockchain and distributed ledger technology, ensuring users have full control over their data and online interactions.

- Openness: Web3 aims to create an equitable digital landscape where everyone can participate, contribute, and benefit from the ecosystem.

- Trustlessness: By utilising cryptographic and consensus mechanisms, Web3 enables trustless interactions between users, eliminating the need for central authorities to validate and authenticate transactions.

- Semantics: Web3 incorporates AI and machine learning to understand data contextually, making it easier for computers to process and analyse information without human intervention.

- Platform Agnosticism: Web3 treats data as pure information, allowing users to choose their preferred means of data consumption, free from platform restrictions.

- Spatiality: Web3 embraces augmented reality (AR) and virtual reality (VR) technologies, enabling users to engage with data and information in immersive, spatial environments.

3.1.3 Key Technologies Enabling Web3

Several emerging technologies and protocols are paving the way for Web3, including:

- Blockchain: Blockchain technology serves as the backbone of decentralised platforms, providing an immutable, transparent, and secure method for recording transactions and data.

- Smart Contracts: Programmable contracts that automatically execute when specific conditions are met, enabling trustless, decentralised applications (dApps) to function without centralised intermediaries.

- Cryptocurrencies: Decentralised digital currencies, such as Bitcoin and Ethereum, provide a means for trustless financial transactions and value transfer within the Web3 ecosystem.

- Decentralised Storage: Solutions like IPFS (InterPlanetary File System) and Filecoin enable decentralised, distributed storage of data, ensuring data persistence and accessibility without relying on centralised servers.

- Decentralised Identity: Blockchain-based identity solutions provide individuals with secure, self-sovereign control over their personal data, enabling crustless authentication and access management.

- Interoperability: Cross-chain protocols, such as Polkadot and Cosmos, facilitate seamless communication and data transfer between different blockchain networks, promoting a cohesive and interconnected Web3 ecosystem.

3.1.4 Challenges and Future Prospects of Web3

While Web3 holds immense promise, several challenges must be addressed to bring this decentralised vision to fruition:

- Scalability: Blockchain networks currently face limitations in transaction throughput and latency, which must be overcome to enable widespread adoption of Web3 applications.

- Security: Decentralised systems must prioritise security measures to prevent potential vulnerabilities and attacks, ensuring the integrity and resilience of the Web3 ecosystem.

- Usability: For mass adoption, Web3 must offer user-friendly interfaces and seamless experiences that rival those of existing centralised platforms.

- Regulation: As decentralised technologies continue to evolve, regulatory frameworks must adapt to accommodate this new paradigm while protecting users and maintaining a fair digital landscape.

- Privacy: While decentralisation inherently promotes increased privacy, Web3 must strike a balance between transparency and protecting user data to prevent potential misuse.

Looking ahead, the future of Web3 is rife with potential as various stakeholders work to address these challenges and refine the underlying technologies. As the concept of Web3 gains traction and becomes more tangible, the transition from the centralised Web 2.0 to a decentralised, user-centric internet will likely reshape the way we interact with information, engage in online transactions, and participate in the digital world.

In conclusion, Web3 represents a significant leap forward in the evolution of the internet, aiming to create a decentralised, open, and trustless digital ecosystem that empowers individuals while addressing the shortcomings of centralised Web 2.0 platforms. Although the realisation of Web3 may still be years away, the underlying technologies and principles are already starting to transform the way we interact with the digital world, ultimately redefining our online experiences and shifting the balance of power from centralised intermediaries back to individual users.

3.2 Virtual Worlds and the Metaverse

The metaverse is rapidly becoming a buzzword in the tech and gaming industries, capturing the attention of both users and developers alike. As an evolution of the internet, the metaverse aims to create a seamless, immersive experience that transcends the boundaries of the digital and physical worlds. In this chapter, we will explore the concept of the metaverse, its current and potential applications,

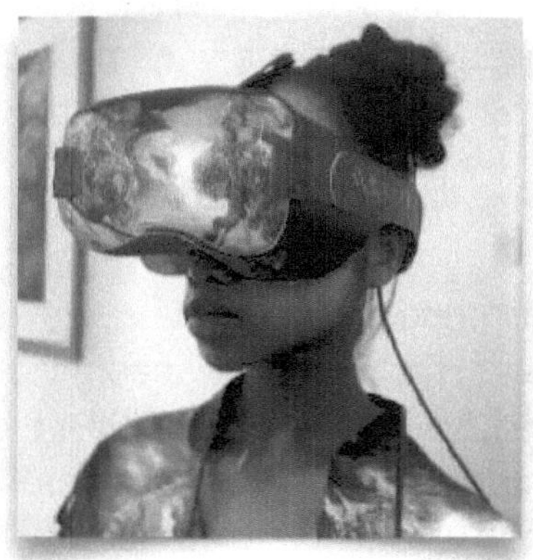

and how businesses and individuals can prepare for this emerging
paradigm.

3.2.1 Defining the Metaverse

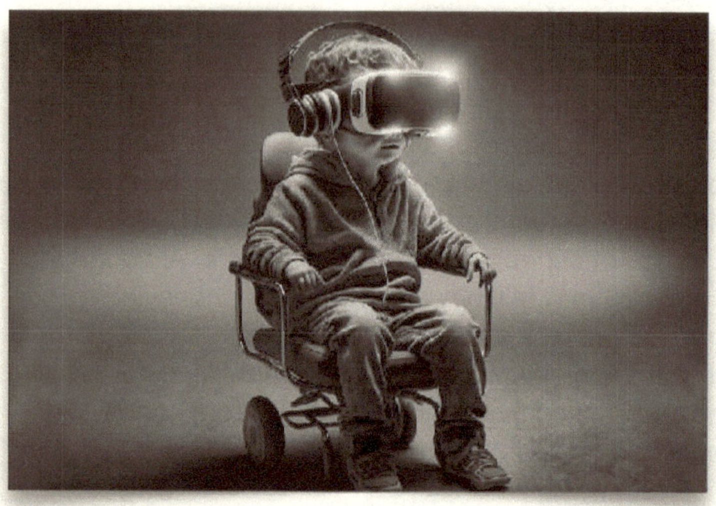

At its core, the metaverse is a collective virtual shared space,
encompassing multiple interconnected digital environments and
experiences. These virtual worlds are accessible through various
platforms and devices, allowing users to interact with each other and
their surroundings in real-time. The metaverse is designed to create a
sense of presence and immersion, simulating the feeling of being
physically present in these digital realms.

3.2.2 The Growing Popularity of the Metaverse

The concept of the metaverse has gained significant traction in recent
years, thanks to advancements in virtual reality (VR), augmented reality
(AR), and mixed reality (MR) technologies. These innovations have
made it possible to create more immersive and interactive experiences,
drawing users into virtual worlds that feel increasingly realistic and
engaging.

Major tech companies like Meta (formerly Facebook), Microsoft, Apple, and Google are investing heavily in the development of metaverse technologies and platforms. These investments are not only driving the growth of the gaming industry but also paving the way for the metaverse to become a mainstream phenomenon. As a result, the metaverse is already impacting various industries, from entertainment and retail to education and healthcare.

3.2.3 Applications of the Metaverse

While the metaverse is currently most associated with gaming, its potential applications extend far beyond entertainment. Here are some examples of how the metaverse could revolutionise various aspects of our lives:

- Work: Remote work and collaboration could be transformed by the metaverse, as employees connect and interact in shared virtual spaces, increasing productivity and fostering a greater sense of camaraderie.

- Education: Virtual classrooms could offer immersive learning experiences, providing students with opportunities to explore and interact with educational content in entirely new ways.

- Retail: Virtual shopping experiences could allow consumers to try on clothes, test out products, or even design custom items, all within the metaverse.

- Socialisation: As the metaverse becomes more accessible, people will be able to forge connections and form communities across the globe, enabling new forms of social interaction and engagement.

- Travel and Tourism: Virtual tourism could offer users the chance to explore far-off destinations and historical sites without leaving their homes, providing an affordable and eco-friendly alternative to traditional travel.

3.2.4 Preparing for the Metaverse

As the metaverse continues to gain traction and influence various aspects of our lives, businesses and individuals must prepare for the changes it will bring. Here are some steps to consider:

1. Stay informed: Keep up-to-date with the latest developments in metaverse technologies, platforms, and trends. This will enable you to anticipate and adapt to the evolving landscape.

2. Develop metaverse skills: Learn about the tools and skills required to create and manage virtual worlds, from 3D modeling and animation to coding and platform management.

3. Embrace new business models: As the metaverse opens up new opportunities for monetisation, businesses must be prepared to adapt their strategies and explore novel revenue streams, such as virtual goods, services, and experiences.

4. Prioritise user experience: In the metaverse, user experience will be paramount. Ensure that your virtual offerings are engaging, intuitive, and immersive to attract and retain users.

In conclusion, the metaverse represents an exciting new frontier in the digital world, offering immense potential for growth and innovation across various industries. As the boundaries between the digital and physical realms continue to blur, the metaverse promises to revolutionise the way we work, learn, socialise, and interact with our environment. By staying informed, developing the necessary skills, and embracing new business models, businesses and individuals can prepare for the emergence of the metaverse and capitalise on the opportunities it presents. As we venture into this new era, the possibilities are virtually limitless, and the metaverse is poised to reshape our world in ways we have yet to imagine.

4. Development Tools and Techniques

4.1 No-code and Low-code Development

The no-code and low-code development movement has emerged as a transformative force in the software industry, offering new opportunities for non-programmers and developers alike to create applications quickly and efficiently. This section explores the evolution of no-code and low-code development, its potential impact on businesses, and its implications for the future of software development.

4.1.1 The Rise of No-code and Low-code Development

The no-code and low-code movement has gained significant traction in recent years, driven by a growing demand for software solutions and a shortage of skilled programmers. Traditional software development requires specialised knowledge of programming languages and extensive experience in software design and engineering. However, with billions of people using office suites like Google Workspace and Office 365, there's a massive untapped potential for creating applications tailored to specific business needs.

No-code and low-code development platforms offer visual drag-and-drop toolsets that enable users to build mobile and web applications by connecting predefined components. Users can create application interfaces by moving UI parts around the screen, write custom logic like Excel functions, and connect their applications to data sources like SharePoint tables or company databases. These platforms empower a new demographic of users – citizen developers – who possess domain expertise and technical skills but lack knowledge of traditional programming languages.

4.1.2 Impact on Businesses and Productivity

No-code and low-code development platforms have the potential to revolutionise the way businesses create and deploy software applications. By enabling non-programmers to develop custom applications, companies can tap into the creativity and domain expertise of their workforce and rapidly prototype and implement solutions to address specific business challenges. Furthermore, these platforms can significantly reduce the time and cost associated with traditional software development, allowing businesses to be more agile and responsive to changing market conditions.

The democratisation of application development can also lead to increased productivity and collaboration within organisations. As employees gain the ability to create and share applications tailored to their needs, they can streamline workflows, automate repetitive tasks, and optimise business processes. In addition, the ease of deployment and sharing of no-code and low-code applications can facilitate cross-functional collaboration and enable teams to work more effectively.

4.1.3 Key Players and Market Growth

Numerous companies have entered the no-code and low-code development market, offering a wide range of tools and platforms catering to different user groups and industries. Microsoft's Power Platform, which includes Power Apps, Power Automate, Power BI, and Power Virtual Agents, is a popular choice for businesses already using Office 365. Other notable platforms include Appian, OutSystems, Salesforce, and Mendix.

Market research firm Gartner estimates that the low-code market will grow to $30 billion by 2025, with low-code application development accounting for 65% of all application development activity by 2024. This rapid growth indicates a strong demand for no-code and low-code solutions and highlights the potential impact of these platforms on the software development landscape.

4.1.4 Future Implications and Challenges

As no-code and low-code development platforms continue to evolve and gain widespread adoption, they will likely reshape the software industry and change the way we think about application development. As more non-programmers become citizen developers, we can expect a surge in innovative applications tailored to specific business needs and industries. This democratisation of software development may also lead to new opportunities for collaboration between professional developers and non-programmers, as well as new business models centred around no-code and low-code solutions.

However, the rise of no-code and low-code development also presents challenges, such as ensuring the security and scalability of applications created using these platforms. Businesses will need to strike a balance between empowering citizen developers and maintaining control over their software ecosystem to minimise risks associated with shadow IT and potential vulnerabilities. Furthermore, as the line between professional developers and citizen developers continues to blur, the role of traditional programmers may need to adapt to incorporate more collaboration, mentorship, and oversight of no-code and low-code development projects.

4.1.5 Integration with Emerging Technologies

The future of no-code and low-code development is not only about empowering more people to create applications, but also about integrating with emerging technologies to unlock new possibilities. Artificial intelligence (AI), machine learning (ML), and the Internet of Things (IoT) are prime examples of technologies that can be leveraged within no-code and low-code platforms to create even more powerful and intelligent applications.

By incorporating AI and ML into no-code and low-code platforms, citizen developers can build applications that leverage data-driven insights and automate complex decision-making processes. This integration can lead to the development of more advanced and sophisticated applications capable of tackling critical business challenges.

Similarly, the integration of IoT technologies with no-code and low-code platforms can enable the development of applications that seamlessly interact with connected devices and sensors, allowing businesses to harness the power of real-time data and build smarter, more efficient systems.

4.1.6 Nurturing a Culture of Innovation

One of the most significant benefits of no-code and low-code development is the opportunity to cultivate a culture of innovation within organisations. By lowering the barriers to entry for application development, employees at all levels can contribute their ideas and expertise to drive business growth and improve operational efficiency.

To fully realise the potential of no-code and low-code development, organisations need to create an environment that encourages experimentation, collaboration, and continuous learning. This involves providing employees with access to the necessary tools and resources, fostering cross-functional communication, and recognising the value of citizen developers as a driving force for innovation.

In conclusion, the no-code and low-code development movement represents a significant shift in the software industry, empowering a new generation of citizen developers to create applications that address specific business needs. By embracing this movement, businesses can unlock new opportunities for innovation, streamline workflows, and drive productivity. As no-code and low-code platforms continue to evolve and integrate with emerging technologies, they will likely play an increasingly critical role in shaping the future of software development.

4.2 Cross-platform Development Tools and Frameworks

In today's technology-driven world, users access applications through a variety of devices and platforms such as Android, iOS, Windows, macOS, and web browsers. Developing an application that runs smoothly across all these platforms can be a daunting task. It often requires expertise in multiple programming languages and continuous maintenance of separate codebases for each platform. This is where cross-platform development tools and frameworks come into play, offering developers the ability to create applications with a single codebase that can be deployed on multiple platforms.

Cross-platform development tools aim to improve resource efficiency by allowing developers to write code once and deploy it on various platforms. Over the years, many cross-platform toolkits have emerged, but not all have stood the test of time. Some, like Appcelerator's

Titanium SDK and PhoneGap (the commercial version of Apache Cordova), have been retired or made available as open-source projects for maintaining existing applications.

As the industry evolves, new cross-platform development tools and frameworks are gaining traction, offering better support and promising futures. Some popular cross-platform development tools and frameworks available today are:

1. React Native: Developed and supported by Facebook, React Native allows developers to create applications using web development technologies like JavaScript, HTML, and CSS. React Native provides pre-built UI components and focuses primarily on iOS and Android platforms. Its  popularity can be attributed to its use of familiar web technologies and the backing of a large organisation like Facebook. https://www.reactnative.dev/

2. Ionic: Similar to React Native, Ionic is an open-source cross-platform development framework that uses web development technologies, including JavaScript, HTML, and CSS. Ionic supports Android, iOS, and Windows platforms, and offers pre-built UI components. The primary difference between Ionic and React Native is the organisation backing them, with Ionic being supported by an open-source organisation.  https://ionicframework.com/

3. Xamarin: Owned and supported by Microsoft, Xamarin is a cross-platform toolkit that allows developers to code in C# using

the .NET framework. Xamarin.Forms, a subset of the project, focuses on user interface development. Xamarin supports Android, iOS, macOS, and Windows platforms, and offers tight integration with Microsoft's Visual Studio development environment. https://dotnet.microsoft.com/en-us/apps/xamarin

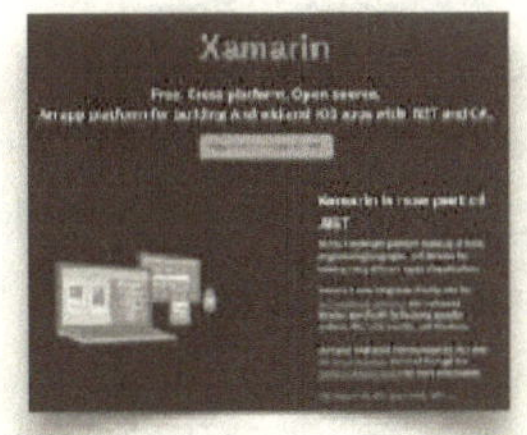

4. Flutter: Created and supported by Google, Flutter is a cross-platform toolkit that uses Dart, a relatively new programming language compared to JavaScript or C#. Flutter enables the development of high-performance applications that can be distributed on Android, iOS, Windows, macOS, the web, and even embedded environments. https://flutter.dev/

Each of these cross-platform development tools and frameworks has its advantages and disadvantages. For instance, React Native and Ionic leverage the existing skills of web developers but may not always provide the same performance and native look and feel as platform-specific applications. On the other hand, Xamarin and Flutter offer higher performance and a more native-like appearance, but may require developers to learn new programming languages and technologies.

When choosing a cross-platform development toolkit, developers must consider factors such as the target platforms, performance requirements, available resources, and the level of trust in the vendors supporting the tools. It is essential to conduct thorough research, experiment with different options, and carefully evaluate the long-term viability of the chosen toolkit.

In conclusion, cross-platform development tools and frameworks have the potential to save time and resources by allowing developers to create and maintain applications with a single codebase across multiple platforms. By selecting the right toolkit for a specific project, developers can minimise the costs and complexities associated with developing and maintaining platform-specific applications, ultimately leading to more efficient and scalable development processes.

Resources:

https://www.reactnative.dev/

https://ionicframework.com/

https://dotnet.microsoft.com/en-us/apps/xamarin

https://flutter.dev/

4.3 Excel and JavaScript

Spreadsheets are an essential tool for businesses and individuals alike, offering a wide range of functionality for data manipulation, analysis, and visualisation. Microsoft Excel is the world's most popular spreadsheet software, and JavaScript is one of the most widely used programming languages. In November 2021, Microsoft announced the integration of JavaScript-based APIs in Excel, which opened up new possibilities for developers and users alike.

4.3.1 Excel and JavaScript: An Unlikely Partnership

At first glance, Excel and JavaScript may seem like an odd combination. Excel is primarily associated with business-oriented tasks, while JavaScript is often linked to web development. However, JavaScript's versatility as a programming language allows it to be used beyond just web pages. By integrating JavaScript APIs in Excel, Microsoft taps into a vast community of developers who can now leverage their skills to create custom data types, functions, and automate tasks within Excel.

4.3.2 Office Scripts and Excel Automation

In 2020, Microsoft introduced a new feature called Office Scripts for users with commercial or educational Office 365 licenses. Office Scripts enables users to record and playback actions in the web-based version of Excel, such as entering data, applying formulas, or formatting output. These recordings are saved in TypeScript, a superset of JavaScript, which can be customised or used to create new scripts from scratch. Although a powerful feature, Office Scripts is limited to certain customers and is only available in the web-based version of Excel, not the desktop versions for Windows or macOS.

4.3.3 Office Add-ins and JavaScript APIs

The JavaScript APIs announced at the 2021 Ignite Conference are designed for use in Office Add-ins – libraries that developers can create and distribute, which work on most platforms where Microsoft Excel is used. Unlike Office Scripts, Office Add-ins are available to all Excel users, irrespective of their licenses or platforms.

Two new JavaScript APIs were introduced:

1. Excel JavaScript API: This API enables developers to access worksheets, ranges, tables, charts, and more using strongly-typed software objects.

2. Common API: This API grants access to features such as user interface elements, dialogues, and client settings.

Microsoft has provided extensive documentation and sample scripts for these new APIs, making it easier for developers to start integrating JavaScript into their Excel projects.

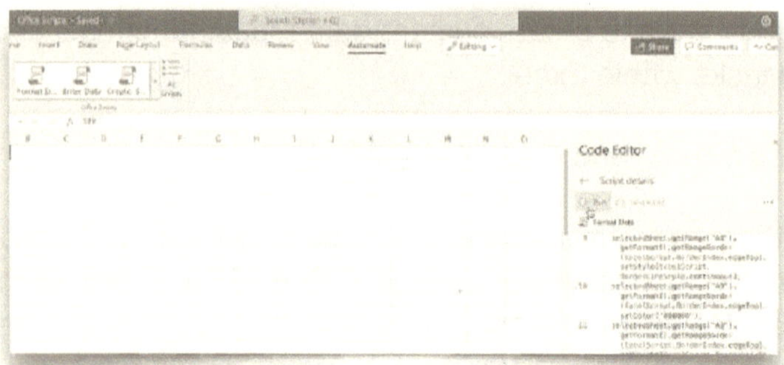

4.3.4 Custom Data Types and Functions

The integration of JavaScript APIs also allows developers to create custom data types that can handle images, arrays, and more. Previously, the API only supported simple values like numbers and strings. Now, developers can define data types that express formatting for these values, allowing them to create reusable formatting rules, such as converting raw numbers to currency-formatted values.

Additionally, developers can define custom functions, expanding the capabilities of Excel even further. While this feature was initially available only in the Windows version of Office, it is expected to expand to other platforms in the future.

4.3.5 Benefits of Excel and JavaScript Integration

The combination of Excel and JavaScript unlocks numerous possibilities for developers and users:

1. Increased functionality: Developers can create custom data types, functions, and automation tools, enhancing Excel's capabilities and offering users more options for data manipulation and analysis.

2. Wider audience: By making Excel accessible to JavaScript developers, Microsoft can tap into a vast pool of talent, encouraging the development of new features and add-ins that benefit all Excel users.

3. Streamlined workflows: The integration of JavaScript APIs enables users to automate repetitive tasks, save time, and improve the overall efficiency of their work processes.

In conclusion, the integration of Excel and JavaScript may seem like an unlikely pairing at first, but by bringing these two technologies together, Microsoft has created a powerful combination that benefits both developers and users. By harnessing the power of a widely popular programming language and the world's leading spreadsheet software, Microsoft has set the stage for an even more feature-rich and versatile tool. The collaboration between Excel and JavaScript has the potential to foster innovative solutions and improve productivity for countless users worldwide.

4.3.6 Future Developments and Opportunities

As Microsoft continues to expand its support for JavaScript within Excel, there are numerous opportunities for developers and users to explore:

1. Cross-platform compatibility: As Microsoft rolls out JavaScript support for Excel across various platforms, developers will have the opportunity to create add-ins and custom functions that work seamlessly on Windows, macOS, and other operating systems.

2. Integration with other Microsoft products: The integration of JavaScript within Excel could pave the way for similar integrations with other Microsoft products, such as PowerPoint and Word, creating a more unified experience across the Office suite.

3. Enhanced collaboration: The ability to share and distribute custom data types, functions, and add-ins among Excel users will promote collaboration and knowledge sharing, ultimately leading to better solutions and more efficient workflows.

4. Improved data visualisation and analysis: As developers create new custom functions and data types, users will have access to more advanced tools for data visualisation and analysis, enabling them to gain deeper insights from their data.

5. Evolving JavaScript APIs: Microsoft is likely to continue refining and expanding the JavaScript APIs for Excel, providing developers with an ever-growing set of tools to enhance the software's capabilities.

6. Community-driven development: As the integration between Excel and JavaScript becomes more widespread, we can expect to see a thriving community of developers sharing their creations, collaborating on new projects, and driving the development of innovative features and add-ins.

By embracing the potential of JavaScript within Excel, Microsoft is charting a course towards a more versatile and powerful spreadsheet tool that can adapt to the needs of a diverse user base. As developers and users continue to explore the possibilities opened up by this integration, we can expect to see an ever-evolving landscape of new features, add-ins, and improvements that will redefine the way we work with spreadsheets.

5. Security and Privacy

5.1 Implementing Zero Trust Security

4.3.1 Introduction to Zero Trust Security

The traditional security model of corporate networks relies on a secure perimeter, where resources are connected to a protected network, and devices within the network are automatically trusted. However, this model has become outdated with the rise of cloud services, mobile devices, remote work, and increasingly sophisticated cyber threats. To adapt to these new challenges, a zero trust security model has emerged, transforming the way organisations approach network security. In this chapter, we'll explore the zero trust model in detail and discuss its benefits, implementation strategies, and potential future developments.

4.3.2 The Evolution of Network Security

The zero trust security model has evolved over time, driven by several factors that have altered the landscape of network security:

1. Technological advancements: Developments in cloud computing, mobile technology, and the Internet of Things (IoT) have led to an increasingly interconnected world, requiring a more flexible and adaptive approach to security.

2. Changing work environments: The rise of remote work and geographically dispersed teams has made traditional security perimeters less effective, necessitating a more comprehensive approach to securing access to resources.

3. Growing cyber threats: As cybercriminals become more sophisticated and cyberattacks more frequent, organizations must adopt more advanced security measures to protect their networks and sensitive data.

These factors have contributed to the shift from a perimeter-based security model to the zero trust model, which focuses on individual devices, users, services, and interactions.

4.3.3 Principles of Zero Trust Security

The zero trust model is built on several core principles:

1. No implicit trust: In a zero trust environment, devices, users, and resources are never automatically trusted. Instead, they must go through authentication and authorisation processes for each interaction.

2. Mutual authentication: Both the user and the resource must verify each other's identity, ensuring that access is granted only to legitimate entities.

3. Least privilege access: Users should be granted the minimum level of access necessary to perform their tasks, reducing the potential damage caused by compromised credentials or unauthorised access.

4. Microsegmentation: The network is divided into smaller, isolated segments, limiting the potential spread of threats and containing breaches within specific areas.

5. Continuous monitoring and evaluation: Security systems should constantly monitor and evaluate devices, users, and resources for signs of compromise or suspicious activity.

6. Defence in depth: Multiple layers of security are used to protect data and resources, making it more difficult for attackers to penetrate the network.

By incorporating these principles, the zero trust model provides a more robust and comprehensive approach to network security.

4.3.4 Implementing Zero Trust Security

To successfully implement a zero trust security model, organizations must follow several key steps:

1. Assess current security posture: Evaluate the existing security infrastructure and identify areas of vulnerability and potential improvement.

2. Define security requirements: Establish the specific security goals and objectives for the organisation, taking into account factors such as regulatory compliance, data sensitivity, and risk tolerance.

3. Map data flows and dependencies: Understand how data and resources are accessed and used within the organisation, and identify the key components and dependencies of the network.

4. Develop a zero trust architecture: Design a security architecture that incorporates the principles of zero trust, including microsegmentation, least privilege access, and mutual authentication.

5. Implement access controls and identity management: Establish strong access controls and identity management systems to ensure that only authorised users and devices can access protected resources.

6. Monitor and evaluate: Continuously monitor and evaluate the effectiveness of the zero trust model, making adjustments and improvements as needed to maintain a strong security posture.

7. Educate and train employees: Ensure that all employees are aware of the zero trust model and their responsibilities in maintaining network security.

4.3.5 Challenges and Opportunities in Zero Trust Security

4.3.5.1 Overcoming Implementation Challenges

Implementing a zero trust security model can be a complex and resource-intensive process. Organisations may face several challenges, such as:

1. Resistance to change: Employees and stakeholders may be resistant to adopting a new security model, especially if they perceive it as more restrictive or cumbersome.

2. Integration with existing systems: Integrating zero trust principles and technologies with legacy systems and infrastructure can be difficult and time-consuming.

3. Scalability: As organisations grow and their security needs evolve, maintaining a zero trust architecture can become increasingly complex and challenging.

4. Cost: Implementing a zero trust model may require significant investment in new technologies, processes, and employee training.

To overcome these challenges, organisations should develop a clear strategy and roadmap for zero trust implementation, ensure effective communication and buy-in from stakeholders, and continuously evaluate and adjust their approach as needed.

4.3.5.2 Opportunities for the Future of Zero Trust Security

As more organisations adopt the zero trust model, new opportunities and advancements are likely to emerge, including:

1. Artificial intelligence and machine learning: AI and machine learning technologies can be used to enhance the effectiveness of zero trust security systems by analysing vast amounts of data, identifying patterns, and automatically adapting security controls in real-time.

2. Increased collaboration and standardisation: As zero trust becomes more widely adopted, there is an opportunity for increased collaboration and standardisation among organisations, vendors, and security experts, leading to the development of best practices, guidelines, and shared resources.

3. Improved user experience: As zero trust security technologies mature, they may become more seamless and user-friendly,

reducing the perceived burden on users and improving overall
user experience.

4. Expanded applications: The principles of zero trust can be
    applied beyond traditional network security to other areas, such
    as IoT devices, supply chain security, and even physical security.

In conclusion, the zero trust security model is a powerful and adaptable
approach to network security that addresses the challenges posed by
today's rapidly evolving technology landscape. By understanding and
implementing the core principles of zero trust, organisations can
significantly reduce their risk of security breaches and protect their
valuable data and resources. As the model continues to mature and
evolve, it is likely to play an increasingly important role in the future of
cybersecurity.

6. Technology Business and Trends

6.1 Analysing the Global Chip Shortage

Microchips, or chips for short, are the backbone of our modern,
technology-driven world. They are found in a wide range of devices,
from smartphones and computers to vehicles and home appliances.
However, a global chip shortage has emerged, leading to delays in
production and delivery of countless products. This sub-chapter will
explore the reasons behind this shortage, its impact on various
industries, and potential solutions to alleviate the problem.

6.1.1 Causes of the Global Chip Shortage

6.1.1.1 COVID-19 Pandemic and Global Shipping Disruptions

The COVID-19 pandemic significantly disrupted global shipping, causing imbalances in the movement of goods, including chips. Ports around the world experienced backlogs as container ships waited to offload and pick up cargo. With reduced passenger flights, air cargo capacity also dwindled, making it more challenging for products to move across borders.

6.1.1.2 Geographical Concentration of Chip Manufacturing

Most advanced chip manufacturing facilities, also known as fabrication plants or fabs, are located in Europe, the Middle East, and Southeast Asia. This geographic concentration of production makes the supply chain vulnerable to disruptions. Efforts are underway to establish new fabs in the United States and other regions to diversify production, but this will take time due to the complex technology and processes involved in chip manufacturing.

6.1.1.3 Changes in Demand and Ordering Patterns

During the pandemic, many industries, including automotive manufacturers, canceled chip orders in anticipation of reduced demand. As demand rebounded, these manufacturers found themselves at the back of the queue, competing with other industries for limited production capacity. Some organizations have also been accused of over-ordering chips, further exacerbating the supply shortage.

6.1.1.4 Workforce and Capacity Reductions

The pandemic led to illness, closures, and capacity reductions in chip factories, affecting the number of chips produced. These issues extended to the mining and refining operations that supply raw materials, such as silicon, to fabs.

6.2 Impacts of the Chip Shortage

6.2.1 Delays in Production of Consumer Electronics

The chip shortage has resulted in delays for various consumer electronics, from laptops and smartwatches to gaming consoles and televisions. Consumers face longer wait times to purchase these devices.

6.2.2 Automotive Industry

The automotive industry has been heavily affected, with some manufacturers halting production due to the chip shortage. This has led to increased wait times for new vehicles and higher prices for both new and used cars.

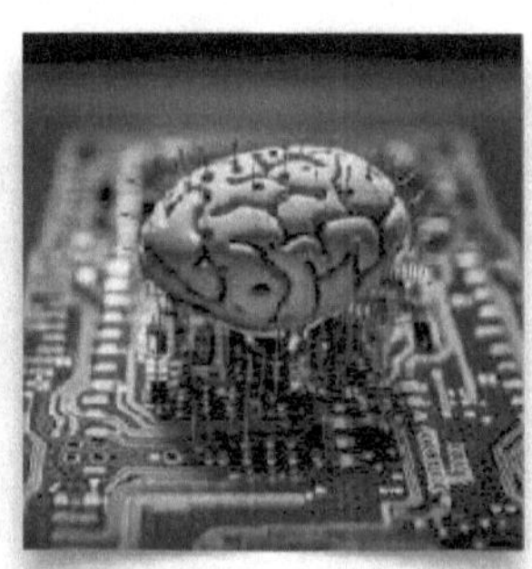

6.2.3 Industrial and Manufacturing Sectors

Chips play a critical role in the operation of machinery and equipment used in various industries, from manufacturing and construction to healthcare and agriculture. The chip shortage has led to production slowdowns and delays in these sectors.

6.2.4 Economic Impact

The global chip shortage has had widespread economic implications, with ripple effects felt throughout supply chains, reduced revenues for affected industries, and potential job losses.

6.3 Potential Solutions and the Future of Chip Manufacturing

6.3.1 Diversification of Chip Production

To reduce the vulnerability of the supply chain, governments and businesses are investing in the construction of new fabs in different regions. This geographical diversification could help alleviate future chip shortages.

6.3.2 Stockpiling and Strategic Reserves

Some have suggested that industries should maintain strategic reserves of chips to guard against future shortages. However, this approach may not be feasible for all industries, as it could lead to increased costs and potential obsolescence.

6.3.3 Technological Innovation

Advancements in chip manufacturing technologies, such as the development of more efficient production processes and alternative materials, could help increase production capacity and reduce the likelihood of future shortages. Additionally, the adoption of new chip designs with greater compatibility and adaptability may ease the transition between different chip models, reducing the impact of shortages on various industries.

6.3.4 Collaboration and Information Sharing

Greater collaboration and information sharing among chip manufacturers, suppliers, and end-users can help create a more transparent and efficient supply chain. This would allow stakeholders to better anticipate and respond to fluctuations in demand and potential disruptions.

6.3.5 Government Support and Policies

Governments can play a critical role in addressing the chip shortage by providing financial incentives for the construction of new fabs and supporting research and development in chip technologies. They can also implement policies to encourage domestic chip production and ensure the availability of essential raw materials.

Conclusion

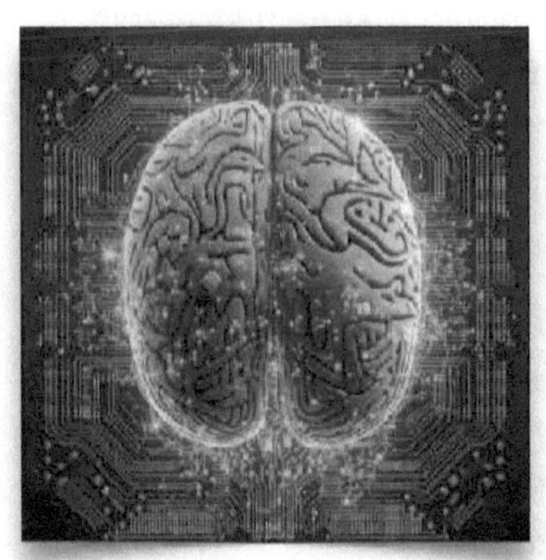

The global chip shortage has exposed the vulnerabilities in the supply chain for these crucial components that power our modern world. While the shortage has had significant economic and industrial impacts, it has also provided an opportunity to address these vulnerabilities and build a more resilient and efficient chip manufacturing ecosystem. By diversifying production, investing in new technologies, fostering collaboration, and implementing supportive government policies, the world can work towards mitigating the risks of future chip shortages and ensuring a steady supply of these essential components.

6.2 Evolving Digital Marketplaces and App Stores

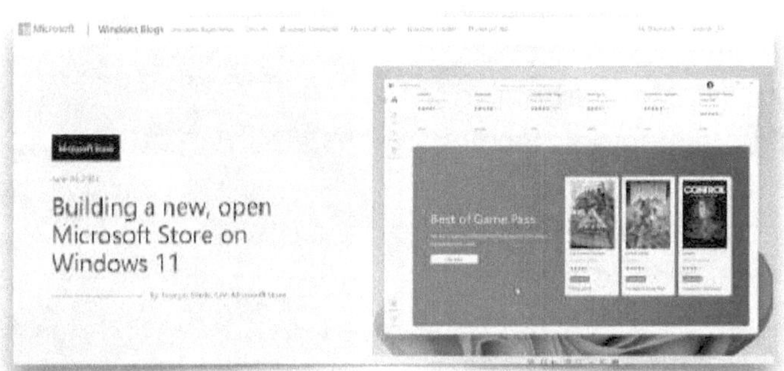

6.2.1 Introduction

The digital marketplace has evolved tremendously over the past few years, with app stores playing a vital role in the distribution of software and applications. Windows, one of the prominent operating systems worldwide, has also made significant improvements in its store, especially with the introduction of Windows 11. This sub-chapter will explore these improvements and analyse the opportunities they present to software developers.

6.2.2 Windows 11 and Microsoft Store Improvements

Windows 11, released in 2021, introduced numerous updates aimed at both consumers and software developers. Some consumer-focused updates include a new user interface and icon sets, while developers benefit from Windows Widgets, a new UI toolkit, and tools for cross-platform development.

The updated Microsoft Store now supports a wide range of application types, making it easier for developers to deploy their applications to Windows, reach a broader audience, and increase revenue potential.

The following sections will delve into the improvements and how they benefit developers.

6.2.3 Support for a Variety of Application Types

The updated Microsoft Store has very few restrictions on the types of applications that can be published. This allows developers to create applications using any framework or packaging technology, leading to a single marketplace for Windows applications. Gone are the days when the Store only contained Universal Windows Platform (UWP) apps. Now, developers can publish WinForms, Windows Presentation Foundation (WPF), C++ Win32 desktop apps, Electron, React Native, Xamarin, Java apps, and Progressive Web Apps (PWAs).

6.2.3.1 Enhanced Installer Packaging

The support for various application types is enabled by the changes to the application installers. Windows 10 had introduced a new installer packaging service called MSIX. With Windows 11, developers can now publish applications based on different installer types, including executables, older MSI installer-based applications, and PWAs.

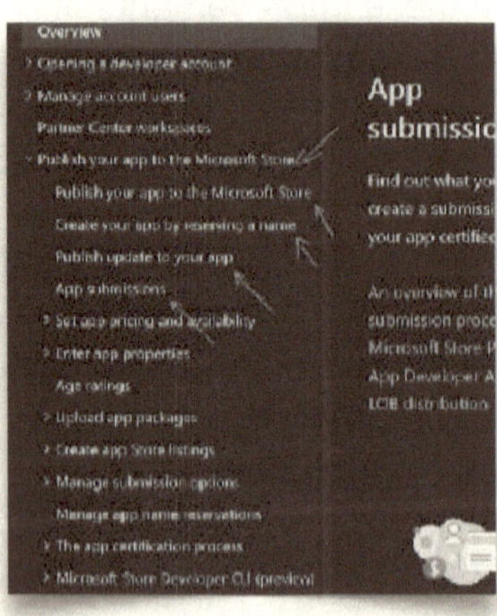

6.2.4 Reaching a Larger Audience

With over one billion users, the Microsoft Store offers developers a vast audience to target. Publishing an app in the Store makes it accessible to consumers around the world, increasing its potential for success.

6.2.5 Revenue Sharing and Commerce Options

Microsoft has updated its revenue sharing policy for the Microsoft Store. Developers can now use their own commerce engines within the interface, allowing them to keep 100% of their revenue. Alternatively, they can choose to use the Microsoft Commerce Service and pay a 15% revenue share for apps or a 12% share for games. The Microsoft Commerce System is robust, globally available, and supports various

revenue streams, making it an attractive option for developers who do not wish to build their own commerce system.

6.2.6 Flagship Desktop Products and Android Apps on Windows

Microsoft has announced its intention to publish all flagship desktop products through the Microsoft Store, including Visual Studio and Microsoft Teams. This move is expected to further boost the Store's credibility and user base. Additionally, Windows 11 allows users to run Android apps on Windows-based computers, enabling Android developers to reach a new audience.

6.2.7 Conclusion

The improvements made to the Microsoft Store with the introduction of Windows 11 provide developers with numerous opportunities to expand their reach, increase revenue, and streamline the deployment process. By supporting a wide variety of application types, offering flexible revenue sharing options, and enabling Android apps on Windows, the evolving digital marketplace demonstrates a commitment to fostering innovation and growth in the software development industry.

Resource:

https://docs.microsoft.com/en-us/windows/uwp/publish

6.3 Cross-platform App Compatibility and Integration

6.3.1 Introduction

The world of software development has seen a rapid shift towards cross-platform compatibility and integration. With the announcement of Windows 11, Microsoft introduced a game-changing feature for Android developers: the ability to run Android apps on Windows-based computers. This sub-chapter will delve into the details of this functionality, its implications, and the steps developers need to take to leverage this opportunity.

6.3.2 Running Android Apps on Windows 11

Windows 11 allows users to run Android apps on their computers, similar to how Google's Chrome OS operates on Chromebooks. These apps can be discovered and installed through a redesigned Windows Store. This new feature opens up a world of possibilities for Android developers, as it bridges the gap between mobile and desktop applications.

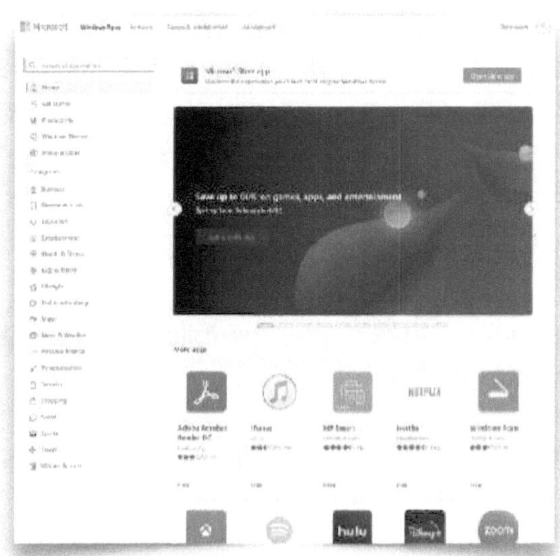

6.3.3 Distribution of Android Apps on Windows

With Windows 11, developers can distribute both universal and conventional desktop applications through the Windows Store, in addition to apps originally built for Android devices. The Windows Store delegates the distribution of Android apps to the Amazon Appstore. When users attempt to install an Android app for the first time, they are prompted to install the Amazon Appstore, which then enables them to install other apps. The Amazon Appstore handles app purchases and provides essential runtime services.

6.3.4 How Android Apps Run on Windows

To understand how Android apps can run on Intel or AMD-based computers, it's essential to know how these apps typically run on Android devices. Android apps are packaged for deployment with the code written in Java or Kotlin, compiled into DEX bytecode. The Android runtime (ART) recompiles this bytecode using ahead-of-time compilation for each device, allowing apps to run on a variety of processors.

On Windows 11 computers and tablets, a technology called the Intel Bridge recompiles the app to work on Intel or AMD processors. This means that apps built with Java or Kotlin should work seamlessly on Windows 11. However, this compatibility is yet to be extensively tested in practice.

6.3.5 Preparing Android Apps for Windows 11

Android developers should consider the following steps to prepare their apps for Windows 11:

1. **Submit apps to the Amazon Appstore**: Until now, the Amazon Appstore was mainly used for Amazon Fire tablets. With Windows 11, the potential customer base expands to the billions of Windows users. Developers should explore submitting their apps to the Amazon Appstore.

2. **Address dependencies on Google Play services**: Apps that rely on Google Play services, such as in-app purchases or the Google Maps API, may need to be rebuilt using Amazon's equivalent tools.

3. **Use build variants**: Developers should learn how to use build variants to create alternative app IDs, multiple versions of resources, and different code paths depending on the installed variant.

4. **Optimise for larger screens**: To ensure apps look and function well on larger screens, developers should create alternate layouts for different screen sizes and manage them with fragments. Apps should adapt gracefully to various screen sizes and pixel

densities to work well on phones, tablets, and full-size computer displays.

5. **Create an Amazon Developer account**: Registering for a free Amazon Developer account allows developers to explore the tools Amazon provides as alternatives to Google Play's APIs, preparing their apps for distribution on Windows 11.

6.3.6 Conclusion

The ability to run Android apps on Windows 11 has the potential to revolutionise cross-platform app compatibility and integration. As a result, Android developers have a unique opportunity to tap into a massive new market by optimising their apps for Windows 11 and the Amazon Appstore. By preparing for this transition and adapting their apps accordingly, developers can leverage the potential of Windows 11 to expand their reach and create a seamless user experience across devices. Embracing this new technology not only benefits developers by broadening their customer base, but also enhances the experience for end-users who can now enjoy a wide variety of Android apps on their Windows devices.

6.3.7 Future Prospects and Challenges

While the integration of Android apps on Windows 11 brings tremendous potential, it also comes with a set of challenges and uncertainties. Developers may face hurdles in adapting their apps to work seamlessly on Windows devices, ensuring consistent performance, and maintaining a high-quality user experience. Moreover, potential differences in security protocols, privacy concerns, and compatibility with Windows-specific features may pose additional challenges.

As the technology advances and evolves, it is crucial for developers to stay informed and adapt their strategies accordingly. The success of this cross-platform integration will largely depend on the ability of developers to tackle these challenges and deliver high-quality, optimised apps for Windows users. As more developers join the Amazon Appstore and optimise their apps for Windows 11, we may witness a paradigm shift in the way apps are developed and distributed across platforms.

6.3.8 The Role of Microsoft and Other Stakeholders

Microsoft plays a crucial role in facilitating the integration of Android apps on Windows 11. Through collaboration with Amazon, they have enabled a new distribution channel and runtime environment for Android apps. To ensure the success of this cross-platform compatibility initiative, Microsoft must continue to invest in the development of tools and resources that support Android developers in their transition to Windows 11.

Other stakeholders, such as Amazon, Intel, and AMD, also have significant roles to play in this new era of app compatibility. They must work closely with Microsoft to ensure seamless compatibility and provide support for developers as they navigate the complexities of optimising their apps for Windows devices.

6.3.9 Final Thoughts

The integration of Android apps on Windows 11 marks a significant milestone in cross-platform app compatibility and integration. As developers seize this opportunity to expand their reach and cater to a broader audience, the software development landscape is poised for a transformative change. By staying ahead of the curve and embracing these advancements, developers can drive innovation and redefine the way we experience apps across devices.

Resource:

https://www.microsoft.com/en-us/store/apps/windows

Appendix A Advanced Prompt Engineering

A.1 Introduction to Prompt Engineering

A.1.1 Definition and importance:

Prompt engineering involves designing and refining inputs to obtain the desired output from a language model. It is important because the quality of the output depends on the input, especially when working with AI models like GPT-4.

Resource: OpenAI's Guide to Prompting - https://platform.openai.com/docs/guides/completion/prompt-design

A.1.2 Overview of language models (e.g., GPT-4) and their applications:

Language models like GPT-4 are pre-trained on vast amounts of text data, learning to generate contextually relevant responses. Applications include chatbots, text summarisation, translation, and more.

Resource: OpenAI Blog - Introducing ChatGPT - https://openai.com/blog/chatgpt/

A.2 Components of Prompt Engineering

A.2.1 Input framing:

Formulating the question or statement in a way that makes the desired information explicit and guides the model to focus on the correct context.

A.2.2 Context setting:

Providing relevant background information to help the model understand the subject matter and produce a more accurate response.

A.2.3 Instructive language:

Using clear and specific instructions to help the model understand what kind of response is expected.

A.2.4 Constraints:

Incorporating constraints like word limits, time frames, or other parameters to help the model focus on relevant information and avoid generating overly long or irrelevant answers.

A.2.5 Iterative refinement:

Continually refining and testing prompts to achieve better results, often through trial and error, by modifying the input or instructions based on the model's output.

A.3 Strategies for Effective Prompt Engineering

A.3.1 Being specific and clear:

Use precise language and clearly state the desired outcome.

A.3.2 Using examples or analogies:

Provide examples or analogies to help guide the model's response.

A.3.3 Incorporating step-by-step instructions or questions:

Break down complex prompts into smaller steps or questions.

A.3.4 Adjusting the level of detail or complexity:

Tailor the prompt to the desired level of detail or complexity.

A.4 Evaluating and Refining Prompts

A.4.1 Analysing model output:

Assess the model's response to determine if it meets the desired criteria.

A.4.2 Identifying issues in the response:

Look for inaccuracies, irrelevancies, or other issues in the output.

A.4.3 Modifying the prompt and testing variations:

Iteratively refine the prompt and test different variations to improve the output.

A.4.4 Learning from successes and failures:

Analyse what worked and what didn't to inform future prompt engineering efforts.

A.5 Challenges and Limitations of Prompt Engineering

A.5.1 Ambiguity and misinterpretation:

Models may misinterpret ambiguous prompts, leading to unexpected responses.

A.5.2 Incomplete or outdated information:

Models may have incomplete or outdated knowledge due to their training data.

A.5.3 Ethical considerations and potential biases:

Models may inadvertently generate biased or offensive content.

Resource:

OpenAI Blog - AI and Compute - https://openai.com/blog/ai-and-compute/

Learn Prompting: https://learnprompting.org/docs/intro

A.5.4 Balancing creativity and control:

Achieving a balance between guiding the model and allowing it to generate creative responses.

A.6 Case Studies and Examples

A.6.1 Real-world applications of prompt engineering:

1. Customer support chatbots: Companies use prompt engineering to train AI chatbots to handle customer queries effectively, ensuring that the bot provides accurate and relevant information in response to user inputs.

2. Content generation: In journalism, social media, or advertising, prompt engineering helps guide AI models to generate creative and contextually appropriate content while minimising the risk of producing irrelevant or offensive material.

3. Text summarisation: AI models are used to summarise long articles, reports, or documents. Prompt engineering ensures that the model captures the essential information and presents it in a concise, coherent manner.

4. Market research analysis: AI models can analyse large volumes of data, such as customer reviews or survey responses. Prompt engineering ensures that the model identifies relevant patterns, trends, or insights in the data.

A.6.2 Comparative analysis of well-crafted vs. poorly designed prompts:

1. Well-crafted prompt: "Please summarise the key findings of the 2021 United Nations Climate Change Report, focusing on the impacts of climate change and suggested mitigation strategies."

   - This prompt is specific, clear, and provides context, guiding the model to produce a focused, relevant summary.

2. Poorly designed prompt: "Tell me about the climate report."

- This prompt is vague and lacks context, making it more likely that the model will produce a less relevant or less informative response.

The differences between well-crafted and poorly designed prompts often lie in the level of specificity, clarity, context, and instruction provided. A well-crafted prompt guides the model to produce a more accurate, relevant, and useful output.

A.6.3 Lessons learned from successful and unsuccessful prompt engineering efforts:

Lessons learned from successful and unsuccessful prompt engineering efforts:

1. Clarity and specificity are crucial: The more specific and clear the prompt, the better the model's output is likely to be. Ambiguity or vagueness can lead to irrelevant or unhelpful responses.

2. Context matters: Providing context helps the model understand the subject matter and produce more accurate responses. Including relevant background information can significantly improve the quality of the output.

3. Instructive language guides the model: Using instructive language, such as asking the model to "list" or "explain," helps set expectations for the type of response desired.

4. Iterative refinement is essential: Continually refining and testing prompts, modifying the input or instructions based on the model's output, is key to achieving better results.

5. Learn from both successes and failures: Analysing what worked and what didn't in previous prompt engineering efforts can help inform future strategies and improve overall performance.

A.6.4 Science, Technology and Mathematics examples of well-crafted vs. poorly designed prompts:

1. Physics

   - Well-crafted prompt: "Explain the principles of classical mechanics using everyday examples."

   - Poorly designed prompt: "Tell me about mechanics."

2. Chemistry

   - Well-crafted prompt: "Describe the process of chemical bonding, including the difference between ionic and covalent bonds."

   - Poorly designed prompt: "Explain bonding."

3. Biology

   - Well-crafted prompt: "Discuss the structure and function of DNA, and explain its role in heredity."

   - Poorly designed prompt: "Talk about DNA."

4. Astronomy

   - Well-crafted prompt: "Explain the significance of the Hubble Space Telescope and its contributions to our understanding of the universe."

   - Poorly designed prompt: "Tell me about a space telescope."

5. Geology

   - Well-crafted prompt: "Describe the process of plate tectonics and its role in the formation of earthquakes and volcanic eruptions."

   - Poorly designed prompt: "Explain how the Earth moves."

6. Environmental Science

   - Well-crafted prompt: "Discuss the causes and consequences of global warming, as well as potential solutions to mitigate its effects."

   - Poorly designed prompt: "Talk about the Earth getting hotter."

7. Computer Science

   - Well-crafted prompt: "Explain the concept of algorithms and provide an example of a common sorting algorithm."

   - Poorly designed prompt: "Tell me about computer stuff."

8. Artificial Intelligence

   - Well-crafted prompt: "Describe the differences between supervised, unsupervised, and reinforcement learning in the context of machine learning."

   - Poorly designed prompt: "Explain AI learning."

9. Blockchain

   - Well-crafted prompt: "Explain the basic principles of blockchain technology and its potential applications beyond cryptocurrency."

- Poorly designed prompt: "What is blockchain?"

10. Cybersecurity

    - Well-crafted prompt: "Discuss the importance of encryption in cybersecurity and provide an example of a widely used encryption method."

    - Poorly designed prompt: "Tell me about security and codes."

11. IoT

    - Well-crafted prompt: "Describe the concept of the Internet of Things (IoT) and its potential impact on daily life and industry."

    - Poorly designed prompt: "Explain smart things."

12. Robotics

    - Well-crafted prompt: "Discuss the current state of robotics and the potential ethical implications of widespread automation."

    - Poorly designed prompt: "Talk about robots and ethics."

13. Software Development

    - Well-crafted prompt: "Explain the Agile software development methodology and how it differs from the Waterfall model."

    - Poorly designed prompt: "Tell me about making software."

14. Algebra

- Well-crafted prompt: "Describe the process of solving a linear equation with one variable and provide an example."

  - Poorly designed prompt: "Explain math with letters."

15. Calculus

  - Well-crafted prompt: "Discuss the concept of derivatives in calculus and provide an example of their real-world application."

  - Poorly designed prompt: "Explain calculus stuff."

16. Geometry

  - Well-crafted prompt: "Explain the Pythagorean theorem and how it can be used to calculate the length of the sides of a right triangle."

  - Poorly designed prompt: "Tell me about triangles."

17. Number Theory

  - Well-crafted prompt: "Describe prime numbers, their importance in number theory, and provide an example of a prime number."

  - Poorly designed prompt: "Explain special numbers."

18. Probability

- Well-crafted prompt: "Discuss the concept of conditional probability and provide an example of its application in real-life situations."

- Poorly designed prompt: "Tell me about the chances of things."

19. Statistics

- Well-crafted prompt: "Explain the difference between descriptive and inferential statistics, and provide examples of each."

- Poorly designed prompt: "What are stats?"

20. Business Marketing

- Well-crafted prompt: "Discuss the role of content marketing in modern business strategy and provide examples of effective content marketing techniques."

- Poorly designed prompt: "Explain marketing stuff."

21. Finance

- Well-crafted prompt: "Describe the concept of diversification in investment strategy and its importance in managing risk."

- Poorly designed prompt: "Tell me about investing."

22. Management

- Well-crafted prompt: "Explain the main functions of management and provide examples of each in a business context."

- Poorly designed prompt: "What do managers do?"

23. Entrepreneurship

- Well-crafted prompt: "Discuss the process of starting a business, including the importance of market research, planning, and resource management."

- Poorly designed prompt: "How to start a business?"

24. Human Resources

- Well-crafted prompt: "Explain the role of human resource management in employee recruitment, retention, and development."

- Poorly designed prompt: "Talk about people at work."

25. Operations

- Well-crafted prompt: "Describe the importance of supply chain management in ensuring efficient business operations and maintaining a competitive advantage."

- Poorly designed prompt: "Explain getting things done in a company."

A.6.5 Business, History, Arts-Literature, Philosophy and Psychology examples of well-crafted vs. poorly designed prompts:

1. Ancient Civilisations

    - Well-crafted prompt: "Compare and contrast the governmental systems of Ancient Egypt and Mesopotamia."

    - Poorly designed prompt: "Tell me about old civilisations."

2. World Wars

    - Well-crafted prompt: "Discuss the major causes of World War I and its long-lasting effects on international relations."

    - Poorly designed prompt: "Explain a big war."

3. Historical Figures

   - Well-crafted prompt: "Analyse the leadership style of Winston Churchill during World War II and its impact on the outcome of the war."

   - Poorly designed prompt: "Talk about a famous leader."

4. Cultural Movements

   - Well-crafted prompt: "Describe the key characteristics of the Renaissance and its influence on art, science, and politics."

   - Poorly designed prompt: "Explain a time when culture changed."

5. Arts & Literature - Music

   - Well-crafted prompt: "Discuss the evolution of classical music through the Baroque, Classical, and Romantic periods."

   - Poorly designed prompt: "Tell me about old music."

6. Arts & Literature - Visual Arts

   - Well-crafted prompt: "Analyze the impact of Impressionism on the art world and its key artists, such as Claude Monet and Pierre-Auguste Renoir."

   - Poorly designed prompt: "Explain a type of painting."

7. Arts & Literature - Film

- Well-crafted prompt: "Discuss the role of film noir in the evolution of cinema and its influence on modern filmmaking."

  - Poorly designed prompt: "Tell me about old movies."

8. Arts & Literature - Theatre

  - Well-crafted prompt: "Explain the cultural significance of Shakespeare's plays and their continuing relevance today."

  - Poorly designed prompt: "Talk about plays."

9. Arts & Literature - Poetry

  - Well-crafted prompt: "Analyse the use of symbolism in William Blake's 'The Tyger' and discuss its overall theme."

  - Poorly designed prompt: "Explain a poem."

10. Arts & Literature - Novels

  - Well-crafted prompt: "Discuss the major themes and narrative techniques in F. Scott Fitzgerald's 'The Great Gatsby.'"

  - Poorly designed prompt: "Tell me about a famous book."

11. Arts & Literature - Literary Analysis

  - Well-crafted prompt: "Explain the concept of the 'unreliable narrator' and provide an example from a well-known literary work."

  - Poorly designed prompt: "What's a narrator?"

12. Philosophy - Ethics

- Well-crafted prompt: "Discuss the differences between consequentialism and deontological ethics, providing examples of each approach."

- Poorly designed prompt: "Explain good and bad."

13. Philosophy - Metaphysics

- Well-crafted prompt: "Explain the concept of determinism and its implications for free will."

- Poorly designed prompt: "Tell me about fate."

14. Philosophy - Epistemology

- Well-crafted prompt: "Discuss the role of skepticism in the development of epistemological theories and its impact on the search for knowledge."

- Poorly designed prompt: "Explain knowing stuff."

15. Philosophy - Political Philosophy

- Well-crafted prompt: "Compare and contrast the political philosophies of John Locke and Thomas Hobbes, focusing on their views of human nature and the role of government."

- Poorly designed prompt: "Talk about old political ideas."

16. Philosophy - Aesthetics

- Well-crafted prompt: "Discuss the concept of beauty in the context of aesthetic philosophy and how different cultures and time periods have defined it."

- Poorly designed prompt: "Explain pretty things."

17. Cognitive Psychology

- Well-crafted prompt: "Explain the process of memory encoding, storage, and retrieval, and discuss factors that can influence memory accuracy."

- Poorly designed prompt: "Tell me about remembering things."

18. Behavioural Psychology

- Well-crafted prompt: "Discuss the principles of operant conditioning, including positive and negative reinforcement, as well as positive and negative punishment."

- Poorly designed prompt: "Explain rewards and punishment."

19. Developmental Psychology

- Well-crafted prompt: "Describe the stages of cognitive development according to Jean Piaget and provide examples of the types of learning that occur at each stage."

- Poorly designed prompt: "Talk about growing up."

20. Social Psychology

- Well-crafted prompt: "Explain the concept of cognitive dissonance and its role in shaping attitudes and behaviour."

- Poorly designed prompt: "Why do people change their minds?"

21. Sociology - Culture

- Well-crafted prompt: "Discuss the concept of cultural relativism and its implications for understanding and evaluating different societies and practices."

- Poorly designed prompt: "Explain different cultures."

22. Sociology - Social Institutions

- Well-crafted prompt: "Analyse the functions and importance of social institutions, such as family, education, and religion, in maintaining social order."

- Poorly designed prompt: "Tell me about society."

23. Sociology - Social Theory

- Well-crafted prompt: "Compare and contrast the sociological perspectives of functionalism, conflict theory, and symbolic interactionism."

- Poorly designed prompt: "Explain theories about people."

24. Sociology - Social Issues

- Well-crafted prompt: "Discuss the factors contributing to income inequality in modern societies and potential solutions to address this issue."

- Poorly designed prompt: "Why are people poor?"

25. Sociology - Globalisation

- Well-crafted prompt: "Analyse the positive and negative effects of globalisation on culture, economy, and the environment."

- Poorly designed prompt: "Explain the world getting smaller."

26. Health & Medicine - Nutrition

- Well-crafted prompt: "Discuss the importance of a balanced diet and the role of different macronutrients (protein, carbohydrates, and fats) in maintaining optimal health."

- Poorly designed prompt: "Tell me about eating right."

27. Health & Medicine - Fitness

- Well-crafted prompt: "Explain the benefits of regular physical activity for mental and physical health, and provide examples of different types of exercises."

- Poorly designed prompt: "Talk about exercise."

28. Health & Medicine - Mental Health

- Well-crafted prompt: "Discuss the impact of stress on mental health and provide strategies for managing stress in daily life."

- Poorly designed prompt: "Explain being stressed."

29. Health & Medicine - Anatomy

- Well-crafted prompt: "Describe the structure and function of the human respiratory system, including the process of gas exchange."

- Poorly designed prompt: "Tell me about breathing."

30. Health & Medicine - Diseases

- Well-crafted prompt: "Explain the differences between bacterial, viral, and fungal infections, including their respective causes and treatments."

- Poorly designed prompt: "Talk about being sick."

31. Health & Medicine - Medical Treatments

- Well-crafted prompt: "Discuss the role of immunotherapy in cancer treatment and its potential benefits andrisks compared to traditional therapies, such as chemotherapy and radiation."

- Poorly designed prompt: "Explain cancer stuff."

A.6.6 Personal Needs, Travel & Geography, Law & Politics, Education and Hobbies & Interests examples of well-crafted vs. poorly designed prompts:

1. Relationships

    - Well-crafted prompt: "Discuss effective communication strategies for resolving conflicts in romantic relationships."

    - Poorly designed prompt: "Tell me about love problems."

2. Time Management

    - Well-crafted prompt: "Explain the Pomodoro Technique and how it can help improve productivity and time management."

    - Poorly designed prompt: "How to manage time?"

3. Personal Finance

    - Well-crafted prompt: "Discuss the importance of an emergency fund and provide guidelines for building one."

    - Poorly designed prompt: "Tell me about saving money."

4. Career Planning

   - Well-crafted prompt: "Explain the process of creating a strategic career plan, including setting goals, identifying opportunities, and building a professional network."

   - Poorly designed prompt: "How to plan a career?"

5. Self-improvement

   - Well-crafted prompt: "Discuss the benefits of mindfulness meditation and its impact on stress reduction and mental well-being."

   - Poorly designed prompt: "Tell me about meditation."

6. Travel Tips

   - Well-crafted prompt: "Provide a list of essential travel tips for first-time international travellers, including packing, safety, and cultural considerations."

   - Poorly designed prompt: "How to travel?"

7. Destinations

   - Well-crafted prompt: "Describe the unique cultural and natural attractions that make New Zealand a popular travel destination."

   - Poorly designed prompt: "Tell me about a place to visit."

8. Cultures

   - Well-crafted prompt: "Discuss the cultural traditions and customs of Japan, including their tea ceremony and the concept of 'omotenashi' (Japanese hospitality)."

- Poorly designed prompt: "Explain Japanese culture."

9. Landmarks

    - Well-crafted prompt: "Describe the historical significance and architectural features of the Eiffel Tower in Paris, France."

    - Poorly designed prompt: "Tell me about a famous building."

10. Climate

    - Well-crafted prompt: "Explain the main factors that influence the Earth's climate, including solar radiation, greenhouse gases, and ocean currents."

    - Poorly designed prompt: "Why is the weather different?"

11. Geography

    - Well-crafted prompt: "Discuss the physical and human geography of the Amazon rainforest, including its biodiversity, climate, and human impact."

    - Poorly designed prompt: "Tell me about the Amazon."

12. Constitutional Law

    - Well-crafted prompt: "Explain the concept of judicial review and its role in the U.S. constitutional system, including the significance of the Marbury v. Madison case."

    - Poorly designed prompt: "How do courts work?"

13. International Law

- Well-crafted prompt: "Discuss the principles and sources of international law, such as treaties, customary international law, and general principles of law."

- Poorly designed prompt: "Explain laws between countries."

14. Political Systems

- Well-crafted prompt: "Compare and contrast the main features of presidential and parliamentary systems of government, using the United States and the United Kingdom as examples."

- Poorly designed prompt: "Tell me about governments."

15. Elections

- Well-crafted prompt: "Explain the Electoral College system in the United States and discuss its pros and cons as a method for electing the president."

- Poorly designed prompt: "How are presidents chosen?"

16. Political Issues

- Well-crafted prompt: "Discuss the implications of climate change on global politics, including international cooperation, resource allocation, and national security."

- Poorly designed prompt: "Tell me about climate and politics."

17. Learning Strategies

- Well-crafted prompt: "Explain the concept of spaced repetition and its effectiveness in enhancing long-term memory retention."

- Poorly designed prompt: "How to learn better?"

18. Curriculum

- Well-crafted prompt: "Discuss the advantages and disadvantages of a standardised curriculum in K-12 education, including its impact on student learning and teacher autonomy."

- Poorly designed prompt: "Explain school subjects."

19. Online Learning

- Well-crafted prompt: "Describe the key features of effective online learning environments, including student engagement, feedback, and assessment."

- Poorly designed prompt: "Tell me about learning on the internet."

20. Teaching Methods

- Well-crafted prompt: "Compare and contrast the teacher-centred and student-centred approaches to teaching, including the benefits and drawbacks of each method."

- Poorly designed prompt: "Explain teaching styles."

21. Education Policy

- Well-crafted prompt: "Discuss the role of standardised testing in education policy and its impact on student performance and teacher accountability."

- Poorly designed prompt: "Tell me about school tests."

22. Sports

- Well-crafted prompt: "Explain the basic rules and gameplay of American football, including scoring, positions, and penalties."

- Poorly designed prompt: "How to play sports?"

23. Cooking

- Well-crafted prompt: "Provide a step-by-step guide to preparing a traditional Italian pasta dish, such as spaghetti carbonara."

- Poorly designed prompt: "Tell me a recipe."

24. Gardening

- Well-crafted prompt: "Discuss the benefits of companion planting and provide examples of compatible plant pairings for a vegetable garden."

- Poorly designed prompt: "Explain plants growing together."

25. DIY

- Well-crafted prompt: "Describe the process of refinishing a wooden table, including the necessary materials, tools, and safety precautions."

- Poorly designed prompt: "How to fix a table?"

26. Board Games

- Well-crafted prompt: "Explain the rules and strategies for playing the board game Settlers of Catan."

- Poorly designed prompt: "Tell me about a game."

27. Collecting

- Well-crafted prompt: "Discuss the history, value, and factors to consider when collecting vintage comic books."

- Poorly designed prompt: "Explain old comics."

28. Crafting

- Well-crafted prompt: "Provide a step-by-step tutorial for creating a macramé plant hanger, including materials, knots, and finishing techniques."

- Poorly designed prompt: "How to make a thing?"

Well-crafted prompts are specific, clear, and provide context, which guides the AI model to produce more detailed, accurate, and helpful responses. In contrast, poorly designed prompts are vague, lack context, and can lead to less informative or accurate responses.

A.7 Conclusion and Future Directions

A.7.1 The evolving role of prompt engineering in AI development:

As AI models become more sophisticated, prompt engineering will continue to play a critical role in obtaining useful and relevant outputs from these models.

A.7.2 Anticipated advancements in language models and their impact on prompt engineering:

Future advancements in AI, such as improved understanding of context and reduced biases, will likely enhance the effectiveness of prompt engineering techniques, making it easier to obtain accurate and relevant responses.

Appendix B Languages Cheat Sheet

B1. Python Cheat sheet

This Python cheat sheet provides you with the basics of Python programming, from variables and data types to classes, OOP, and event-driven programming. Keep practicing and exploring the language to become proficient in Python.


```python
# Variables
a = 5  # Integer
b = 3.14  # Float
c = "Hello"  # String

# Constants (by convention, uppercase)
PI = 3.14159
```



```python
# Lists
my_list = [1, 2, 3]
my_list.append(4)

# Tuples (immutable)
my_tuple = (1, 2, 3)

# Sets (unordered, unique elements)
my_set = {1, 2, 3}
my_set.add(4)

# Dictionaries
my_dict = {"key1": "value1", "key2": "value2"}
my_dict["key3"] = "value3"
```

Basic Operations

```python
a = 5 + 2  # Addition
b = 5 - 2  # Subtraction
c = 5 * 2  # Multiplication
d = 5 / 2  # Division
e = 5 % 2  # Modulus
f = 5 ** 2  # Exponent
g = 5 // 2  # Floor division
```

Control Flow

```python
# If
if a < b:
    print("a is less than b")
elif a == b:
    print("a is equal to b")
else:
    print("a is greater than b")

# Switch (use a dictionary to mimic switch-case)
def case1():
    return "Case 1"
def case2():
    return "Case 2"

switch = {
    1: case1,
    2: case2
}

result = switch.get(value, lambda: "Default case")()

# Loops
for i in range(5):  # Range from 0 to 4
    print(i)

while a < b:
    print(a)
    a += 1
```

```python
def add(a, b):
    return a + b

result = add(5, 3)
```



```python
# Creating a module (e.g., my_module.py)
def hello():
    return "Hello, World!"

# Using a module
import my_module
print(my_module.hello())

# Importing specific functions
from my_module import hello
print(hello())

# Aliasing a module
import my_module as mm
print(mm.hello())
```



```python
import math
import os
import sys
import datetime
import random
import re
import json
import requests
import numpy
import pandas
import matplotlib.pyplot as plt
```

Classes

```python
class MyClass:
    def __init__(self, a, b):
        self.a = a
        self.b = b

    def add(self):
        return self.a + self.b


my_instance = MyClass(5, 3)
result = my_instance.add()
```

Object-Oriented Programming

```python
# Inheritance
class ChildClass(MyClass):
    def multiply(self):
        return self.a * self.b


child_instance = ChildClass(5, 3)
result = child_instance.multiply()

# Polymorphism (method overriding)
class Animal:
    def speak(self):
        pass
class Dog(Animal):
    def speak(self):
        return "Woof!"
class Cat(Animal):
    def speak(self):
        return "Meow!"
```

Event-Driven Programming

```python
# Use the 'tkinter' library for simple event-driven programming
import tkinter as tk

def on_button_click():
    print("Button clicked")

app = tk.Tk()
button = tk.Button(app, text="Click me", command=on_button_click)
button.pack()
app.mainloop()
```

B2. JavaScript Cheat sheet

This JavaScript cheat sheet provides you with the basics of JavaScript programming, from variables and data types to classes, OOP, and event-driven programming. Keep practicing and exploring the language to become proficient in JavaScript. Make use of the vast library of npm packages available to expand your skillset and build more complex applications.

Variables/Constants and Types

```
// Variables
let a = 5; // Number
let b = 3.14; // Number
let c = "Hello"; // String

// Constants
const PI = 3.14159;
```

Data types

```
// Arrays
let myArray = [1, 2, 3];
myArray.push(4);

// Objects
let myObject = {
  key1: "value1",
  key2: "value2"
};
myObject.key3 = "value3";
```

Basic Operations

```
let a = 5 + 2; // Addition
let b = 5 - 2; // Subtraction
let c = 5 * 2; // Multiplication
let d = 5 / 2; // Division
let e = 5 % 2; // Modulus
let f = 5 ** 2; // Exponent
```

```javascript
// If
if (a < b) {
  console.log("a is less than b");
} else if (a === b) {
  console.log("a is equal to b");
} else {
  console.log("a is greater than b");
}

// Switch
switch (value) {
  case 1:
    console.log("Case 1");
    break;
  case 2:
    console.log("Case 2");
    break;
  default:
    console.log("Default case");
}

// Loops
for (let i = 0; i < 5; i++) {
  console.log(i);
}

while (a < b) {
  console.log(a);
  a++;
}
```



```javascript
function add(a, b) {
  return a + b;
}

let result = add(5, 3);
```

Modules

```javascript
// Exporting (myModule.js)
export function hello() {
  return "Hello, World!";
}

// Importing
import { hello } from "./myModule.js";
console.log(hello());
```

Useful and most important modules

JavaScript has a vast ecosystem, primarily in the form of npm packages. Some popular npm packages include:
- lodash
- moment
- axios
- express
- react
- angular
- vue
- jquery

Classes

```javascript
class MyClass {
  constructor(a, b) {
    this.a = a;
    this.b = b;
  }

  add() {
    return this.a + this.b;
  }
}

let myInstance = new MyClass(5, 3);
let result = myInstance.add();
```

```javascript
// Inheritance
class ChildClass extends MyClass {
  multiply() {
    return this.a * this.b;
  }
}

let childInstance = new ChildClass(5, 3);
let result = childInstance.multiply();

// Polymorphism (method overriding)
class Animal {
  speak() {
    return "";
  }
}

class Dog extends Animal {
  speak() {
    return "Woof!";
  }
}

class Cat extends Animal {
  speak() {
    return "Meow!";
  }
}
```



```javascript
// Add an event listener to an element (e.g., button)
document.querySelector("#myButton").addEventListener("click", () => {
  console.log("Button clicked");
});
```

B3. Java Cheat sheet

This Java cheat sheet provides you with the basics of Java programming, from variables and data types to classes, OOP, and event-driven programming. Keep practicing and exploring the language to become proficient in Java.

Variables/Constants and Types

```java
// Variables
int a = 5; // Integer
double b = 3.14; // Double
String c = "Hello"; // String

// Constants
final double PI = 3.14159;
```

Data types

```java
// Arrays
int[] myArray = {1, 2, 3};
myArray[3] = 4;

// ArrayList (dynamic)
import java.util.ArrayList;
ArrayList<Integer> myList = new ArrayList<>();
myList.add(1);

// HashMap
import java.util.HashMap;
HashMap<String, String> myMap = new HashMap<>();
myMap.put("key1", "value1");
```

Basic Operations

```java
int a = 5 + 2; // Addition
int b = 5 - 2; // Subtraction
int c = 5 * 2; // Multiplication
double d = 5.0 / 2.0; // Division
int e = 5 % 2; // Modulus
double f = Math.pow(5, 2); // Exponent
```

```java
// If
if (a < b) {
    System.out.println("a is less than b");
} else if (a == b) {
    System.out.println("a is equal to b");
} else {
    System.out.println("a is greater than b");
}

// Switch
switch (value) {
    case 1:
        System.out.println("Case 1");
        break;
    case 2:
        System.out.println("Case 2");
        break;
    default:
        System.out.println("Default case");
}

// Loops
for (int i = 0; i < 5; i++) {
    System.out.println(i);
}

while (a < b) {
    System.out.println(a);
    a++;
}
```



```java
public static int add(int a, int b) {
    return a + b;
}

int result = add(5, 3);
```

```java
// Create a package (folder) with a class (MyClass.java)
package mypackage;

public class MyClass {
    public static String hello() {
        return "Hello, World!";
    }
}

// Import and use the package
import mypackage.MyClass;

public class Main {
    public static void main(String[] args) {
        System.out.println(MyClass.hello());
    }
}
```


- java.util (Collections, Date, etc.)
- java.io (File I/O)
- java.nio (Non-blocking I/O)
- java.net (Networking)
- java.math (BigDecimal, BigInteger)
- javax.swing (GUI)

```java
public class MyClass {
   private int a;
   private int b;

   public MyClass(int a, int b) {
      this.a = a;
      this.b = b;
   }
   public int add() {
      return this.a + this.b;
   }
}
MyClass myInstance = new MyClass(5, 3);
int result = myInstance.add();
```



```java
// Inheritance
public class ChildClass extends MyClass {
   public int multiply() {
      return this.a * this.b;
   }
}
ChildClass childInstance = new ChildClass(5, 3);
int result = childInstance.multiply();
// Polymorphism (method overriding)
abstract class Animal {
   public abstract String speak();
}
class Dog extends Animal {
public String speak() {
return "Woof!";
}
}
class Cat extends Animal {
public String speak() {
return "Meow!";
}
}
```

```java
// Java Swing and JavaFX are popular libraries for creating GUI applications
with event-driven programming.
// Java Swing example
import javax.swing.*;
import java.awt.event.ActionEvent;
import java.awt.event.ActionListener;

public class Main {
    public static void main(String[] args) {
        JFrame frame = new JFrame("Event-Driven Programming");
        JButton button = new JButton("Click me");

        button.addActionListener(new ActionListener() {
          @Override
          public void actionPerformed(ActionEvent e) {
             System.out.println("Button clicked");
          }
        });

        frame.getContentPane().add(button);
        frame.setDefaultCloseOperation(JFrame.EXIT_ON_CLOSE);
        frame.setSize(300, 200);
        frame.setVisible(true);
    }
}
```

B4. Swift Cheat sheet

This Swift cheat sheet provides you with the basics of Swift programming, from variables and data types to classes, OOP, and event-driven programming. Keep practicing and exploring the language to become proficient in Swift, especially for iOS development.

Data types

```swift
// Arrays
var myArray = [1, 2, 3]
myArray.append(4)

// Dictionaries
var myDict: [String: String] = ["key1": "value1", "key2": "value2"]
myDict["key3"] = "value3"
```

Basic Operations

```swift
let a = 5 + 2 // Addition
let b = 5 - 2 // Subtraction
let c = 5 * 2 // Multiplication
let d = 5 / 2 // Division
let e = 5 % 2 // Modulus
let f = pow(5, 2) // Exponent
```

Functions

```swift
func add(_ a: Int, _ b: Int) -> Int {
    return a + b
}

let result = add(5, 3)
```

```swift
// If
if a < b {
    print("a is less than b")
} else if a == b {
    print("a is equal to b")
} else {
    print("a is greater than b")
}
// Switch
switch value {
case 1:
    print("Case 1")
case 2:
    print("Case 2")
default:
    print("Default case")
}
// Loops
for i in 0..<5 {
    print(i)
}
while a < b {
    print(a)
    a += 1
}
```



```swift
// Import a framework
import UIKit
```

- UIKit (iOS user interface)
- Foundation (basic functionality)
- CoreGraphics (2D graphics)
- CoreAnimation (animations)
- CoreData (data persistence)
- CoreLocation (location services)
- MapKit (maps)
- Alamofire (HTTP networking)

Classes

```swift
class MyClass {
    var a: Int
    var b: Int

    init(a: Int, b: Int) {
        self.a = a
        self.b = b
    }

    func add() -> Int {
        return a + b
    }
}

let myInstance = MyClass(a: 5, b: 3)
let result = myInstance.add()
```

```swift
// Inheritance
class ChildClass: MyClass {
   func multiply() -> Int {
      return a * b
   }
}

let childInstance = ChildClass(a: 5, b: 3)
let result = childInstance.multiply()

// Polymorphism (method overriding)
class Animal {
   func speak() -> String {
      return ""
   }
}

class Dog: Animal {
   override func speak() -> String {
      return "Woof!"
   }
}

class Cat: Animal {
   override func speak() -> String {
      return "Meow!"
   }
}
```

```swift
//Swift is commonly used for iOS development, which is inherently event-
driven. The UIKit and SwiftUI frameworks provide tools to create event-
driven applications for Apple platforms.

import UIKit

class MyViewController: UIViewController {
   override func viewDidLoad() {
     super.viewDidLoad()

     let button = UIButton(type: .system)
     button.setTitle("Click me", for: .normal)
     button.addTarget(self, action: #selector(onButtonClick),
for: .touchUpInside)
     button.frame = CGRect(x: 100, y: 100, width: 200, height: 40)
     view.addSubview(button)
   }

   @objc func onButtonClick() {
     print("Button clicked")
   }
}

// In SceneDelegate.swift, set the root view controller to MyViewController
func scene(_ scene: UIScene, willConnectTo session: UISceneSession,
options connectionOptions: UIScene.ConnectionOptions) {
   guard let windowScene = (scene as? UIWindowScene) else { return }

   let window = UIWindow(windowScene: windowScene)
   window.rootViewController = MyViewController()
   window.makeKeyAndVisible()
   self.window = window
}
```

B5. C Cheat sheet

This C cheat sheet provides you with the basics of C programming, from variables and data types to control flow and functions. Keep practicing and exploring the language to become proficient in C.

Variables/Constants and Types

```c
// Variables
int a = 5; // Integer
double b = 3.14; // Double
char c[] = "Hello"; // String

// Constants
const double PI = 3.14159;
```

Data types

```c
// Arrays
int myArray[] = {1, 2, 3};
myArray[3] = 4;

// Structs
struct Person {
    char name[50];
    int age;
};

struct Person p = {"John", 30};
```

Basic Operations

```c
int a = 5 + 2; // Addition
int b = 5 - 2; // Subtraction
int c = 5 * 2; // Multiplication
double d = 5.0 / 2.0; // Division
int e = 5 % 2; // Modulus
double f = pow(5, 2); // Exponent
```

Control Flow

```c
// If
if (a < b) {
    printf("a is less than b");
} else if (a == b) {
    printf("a is equal to b");
} else {
    printf("a is greater than b");
}

// Switch
switch (value) {
    case 1:
        printf("Case 1");
        break;
    case 2:
        printf("Case 2");
        break;
    default:
        printf("Default case");
}

// Loops
for (int i = 0; i < 5; i++) {
    printf("%d\n", i);
}

while (a < b) {
    printf("%d\n", a);
    a++;
}
```

Functions

```c
int add(int a, int b) {
    return a + b;
}

int result = add(5, 3);
```

Modules

```c
// Create a header file (my_module.h)
#ifndef MY_MODULE_H
#define MY_MODULE_H

int add(int a, int b);

#endif

// Create a source file (my_module.c)
#include "my_module.h"

int add(int a, int b) {
    return a + b;
}

// Include and use the module
#include "my_module.h"

int main() {
    printf("%d\n", add(5, 3));
    return 0;
}
```

- stdio.h (standard input/output)
- stdlib.h (general utilities)
- string.h (string manipulation)
- math.h (math functions)
- time.h (time functions)
- ctype.h (character functions)

C is a procedural language and does not have built-in support for classes and OOP features..

B6. C++ Cheat sheet

This C++ cheat sheet provides you with the basics of C++ programming, from variables and data types to classes, OOP, and event-driven programming. Keep practicing and exploring the language to become proficient in C++.

Variables/Constants and Types

```cpp
// Variables
int a = 5; // Integer
double b = 3.14; // Double
std::string c = "Hello"; // String

// Constants
const double PI = 3.14159;
```

Data types

```cpp
// Arrays
int myArray[] = {1, 2, 3};
myArray[3] = 4;

// Vectors
std::vector<int> myVector = {1, 2, 3};
myVector.push_back(4);
```

Basic Operations

```cpp
int a = 5 + 2; // Addition
int b = 5 - 2; // Subtraction
int c = 5 * 2; // Multiplication
double d = 5.0 / 2.0; // Division
int e = 5 % 2; // Modulus
double f = pow(5, 2); // Exponent
```

```cpp
// If
if (a < b) {
   std::cout << "a is less than b";
} else if (a == b) {
   std::cout << "a is equal to b";
} else {
   std::cout << "a is greater than b";
}

// Switch
switch (value) {
   case 1:
      std::cout << "Case 1";
      break;
   case 2:
      std::cout << "Case 2";
      break;
   default:
      std::cout << "Default case";
}

// Loops
for (int i = 0; i < 5; i++) {
   std::cout << i << std::endl;
}

while (a < b) {
   std::cout << a << std::endl;
   a++;
}
```

```cpp
int add(int a, int b) {
    return a + b;
}


int result = add(5, 3);
```

Modules - Header Files in C++

```cpp
// Create a header file (my_module.hpp)
#ifndef MY_MODULE_HPP
#define MY_MODULE_HPP

int add(int a, int b);
#endif
// Create a source file (my_module.cpp)
#include "my_module.hpp"

int add(int a, int b) {
    return a + b;
}
// Include and use the module
#include "my_module.hpp"
int main() {
    std::cout << add(5, 3) << std::endl;
    return 0;
}
```

Useful and most important modules - libraries

- iostream (input/output streams)
- fstream (file input/output)
- string (strings)
- vector (dynamic arrays)
- algorithm (algorithms)
- cmath (math functions)
- chrono (time functions)

```cpp
class MyClass {
public:
   int a;
   int b;
   MyClass(int a, int b) {
      this->a = a;
      this->b = b;
   }
   int add() {
      return a + b;
   }
};
MyClass myInstance(5, 3);
int result = myInstance.add();
```


//C++ does not have built-in support for EDP. However, you can use libraries like Boost.Asio, libevent, or libuv to handle events in a C++ program. Below is an example using the Boost.Asio library:

```cpp
#include <iostream>
#include <boost/asio.hpp>

void on_timer(const boost::system::error_code&) {
   std::cout << "Hello, world!" << std::endl;
}

int main() {
   boost::asio::io_context io;
   boost::asio::steady_timer timer(io, boost::asio::chrono::seconds(5));
   timer.async_wait(&on_timer);
   io.run();
   return 0;
}
```

```cpp
// Inheritance
class ParentClass {
public:
   int a;
   int b;

   ParentClass(int a, int b) {
     this->a = a;
     this->b = b;
   }

   int add() {
     return a + b;
   }
};

class ChildClass : public ParentClass {
public:
   ChildClass(int a, int b) : ParentClass(a, b) {}
   int multiply() {
     return a * b;
   }
};

ChildClass childInstance(5, 3);
int result = childInstance.multiply();

// Polymorphism
class Animal {
public:
   virtual std::string speak() = 0;
};

class Dog : public Animal {
public:
   std::string speak() override {
     return "Woof!";
   }
};

class Cat : public Animal {
public:
   std::string speak() override {
     return "Meow!";
   }
};

Animal* myAnimal = new Dog();
```

B7. C# Cheat sheet

This C# cheat sheet provides you with the basics of C# programming, from variables and data types to classes, OOP, and event-driven programming. Keep practicing and exploring the language to become proficient in C#.

Variables/Constants and Types

```
// Variables
int a = 5; // Integer
double b = 3.14; // Double
string c = "Hello"; // String

// Constants
const double PI = 3.14159;
```

Data types

```
// Arrays
int[] myArray = {1, 2, 3};
myArray[3] = 4;

// Lists
List<int> myList = new List<int> {1, 2, 3};
myList.Add(4);
```

Basic Operations

```
int a = 5 + 2; // Addition
int b = 5 - 2; // Subtraction
int c = 5 * 2; // Multiplication
double d = 5.0 / 2.0; // Division
int e = 5 % 2; // Modulus
double f = Math.Pow(5, 2); // Exponent
```

```csharp
// If
if (a < b) {
    Console.WriteLine("a is less than b");
} else if (a == b) {
    Console.WriteLine("a is equal to b");
} else {
    Console.WriteLine("a is greater than b");
}

// Switch
switch (value) {
    case 1:
        Console.WriteLine("Case 1");
        break;
    case 2:
        Console.WriteLine("Case 2");
        break;
    default:
        Console.WriteLine("Default case");
}

// Loops
for (int i = 0; i < 5; i++) {
    Console.WriteLine(i);
}

while (a < b) {
    Console.WriteLine(a);
    a++;
}
```

```
int Add(int a, int b) {
    return a + b;
}

int result = Add(5, 3);
```

Modules -Namespaces in C#

```
// Create a module (MyModule.cs)
namespace MyModule {
    public class MyCalculator {
        public int Add(int a, int b) {
            return a + b;
        }
    }
}

// Use the module
using MyModule;

MyCalculator calc = new MyCalculator();
Console.WriteLine(calc.Add(5, 3));
```

Useful and most important modules

- System (core functionality)
- System.IO (file input/output)
- System.Collections.Generic (collections)
- System.Linq (querying)
- System.Text (text manipulation)
- System.Threading.Tasks (multithreading)

```
class MyClass {
   public int a;
   public int b;

   public MyClass(int a, int b) {
      this.a = a;
      this.b = b;
   }

   public int Add() {
      return a + b;
   }
}

MyClass myInstance = new MyClass(5, 3);
int result = myInstance.Add();
```

```csharp
// C# supports event-driven programming using events and delegates.

// Define a custom event arguments class
public class MyEventArgs : EventArgs {
    public string Message { get; set; }
    public MyEventArgs(string message) {
        Message = message;
    }
}

// Define a publisher class with an event
public class MyPublisher {
    public event EventHandler<MyEventArgs> MyEvent;

    public void TriggerEvent(string message) {
        MyEvent?.Invoke(this, new MyEventArgs(message));
    }
}

// Define a subscriber class
public class MySubscriber {
    public void OnMyEvent(object sender, MyEventArgs e) {
        Console.WriteLine($"Event received: {e.Message}");
    }
}

// Example usage
MyPublisher publisher = new MyPublisher();
MySubscriber subscriber = new MySubscriber();

// Subscribe to the event
publisher.MyEvent += subscriber.OnMyEvent;

// Trigger the event
publisher.TriggerEvent("Hello, world!");
```

```csharp
// Inheritance
class ParentClass {
   public int a;
   public int b;

   public ParentClass(int a, int b) {
      this.a = a;
      this.b = b;
   }

   public int Add() {
      return a + b;
   }
}

class ChildClass : ParentClass {
   public ChildClass(int a, int b) : base(a, b) {}
   public int Multiply() {
      return a * b;
   }
}

ChildClass childInstance = new ChildClass(5, 3);
int result = childInstance.Multiply();

// Polymorphism
abstract class Animal {
   public abstract string Speak();
}

class Dog : Animal {
   public override string Speak() {
      return "Woof!";
   }
}

class Cat : Animal {
   public override string Speak() {
      return "Meow!";
   }
}

Animal myAnimal = new Dog();
Console.WriteLine(myAnimal.Speak()); // Output: Woof!
```

B8. Kotlin Cheat sheet

This Kotlin cheat sheet provides you with the basics of Kotlin programming, from variables and data types to classes, OOP, and event-driven programming. Keep practicing and exploring the language to become proficient in Kotlin.

Variables/Constants and Types

```kotlin
// Variables
var a: Int = 5 // Integer
var b: Double = 3.14 // Double
var c: String = "Hello" // String

// Constants (Immutable)
val PI: Double = 3.14159
```

Data types

```kotlin
// Arrays
val myArray = arrayOf(1, 2, 3)
myArray[3] = 4

// Lists
val myList = mutableListOf(1, 2, 3)
myList.add(4)
```

Basic Operations

```kotlin
val a = 5 + 2 // Addition
val b = 5 - 2 // Subtraction
val c = 5 * 2 // Multiplication
val d = 5.0 / 2.0 // Division
val e = 5 % 2 // Modulus
val f = 5.0.pow(2) // Exponent
```

Control Flow

```kotlin
// If
val result = if (a < b) {
    "a is less than b"
} else if (a == b) {
    "a is equal to b"
} else {
    "a is greater than b"
}

// When (Kotlin's version of Switch)
when (value) {
    1 -> println("Case 1")
    2 -> println("Case 2")
    else -> println("Default case")
}

// Loops
for (i in 0 until 5) {
    println(i)
}

while (a < b) {
    println(a)
    a++
}
```

Functions

```kotlin
fun add(a: Int, b: Int): Int {
    return a + b
}

val result = add(5, 3)
```

Modules

```kotlin
// Create a package (MyModule.kt)
package mymodule

fun add(a: Int, b: Int): Int {
    return a + b
}

// Use the package
import mymodule.add

val result = add(5, 3)
```

Useful and most important modules - libraries

```
kotlin.io (file input/output)
kotlin.collections (collections)
kotlin.sequences (lazy sequences)
kotlin.text (text manipulation)
kotlinx.coroutines (coroutines for asynchronous programming)
```

Classes

```kotlin
class MyClass(val a: Int, val b: Int) {
    fun add(): Int {
        return a + b
    }
}

val myInstance = MyClass(5, 3)
val result = myInstance.add()
```

```kotlin
// Inheritance
open class ParentClass(val a: Int, val b: Int) {
   fun add(): Int {
      return a + b
   }
}

class ChildClass(a: Int, b: Int) : ParentClass(a, b) {
   fun multiply(): Int {
      return a * b
   }
}

val childInstance = ChildClass(5, 3)
val result = childInstance.multiply()

// Polymorphism
abstract class Animal {
   abstract fun speak(): String
}

class Dog : Animal() {
   override fun speak(): String {
      return "Woof!"
   }
}

class Cat : Animal() {
   override fun speak(): String {
      return "Meow!"
   }
}

val myAnimal: Animal = Dog()
println(myAnimal.speak()) // Output: Woof!
```

```kotlin
// Kotlin does not have built-in support for EDP. However, you can use
// libraries like kotlinx.coroutines for asynchronous programming or work with
// Android framework (if you're developing Android apps) to handle events.
// Here's a simple example using Kotlin coroutines:

import kotlinx.coroutines.GlobalScope
import kotlinx.coroutines.delay
import kotlinx.coroutines.launch

// Define a class with a listener
class MyEventPublisher {
    private val listeners = mutableListOf<(String) -> Unit>()

    fun addListener(listener: (String) -> Unit) {
        listeners.add(listener)
    }

    suspend fun triggerEvent(message: String) {
        delay(1000) // Simulate async event
        listeners.forEach { it(message) }
    }
}

// Example usage
val publisher = MyEventPublisher()

// Add a listener
publisher.addListener { message -> println("Event received: $message") }

// Trigger the event
GlobalScope.launch {
    publisher.triggerEvent("Hello, world!")
}

// Keep the main thread alive until the event is received
Thread.sleep(2000)
```

Appendix C ChatGPT for Learning Programming Languages

Introduction:

In this appendix, we will explore how to utilise ChatGPT, an advanced
AI language model, to assist you in learning programming languages
and mastering the concept of lambda functions. With its ability to
understand context and provide helpful information, ChatGPT serves
as a valuable resource for learning programming concepts, syntax, and
best practices. We will discuss various ways to use ChatGPT
effectively for enhancing your programming skills and understanding of
lambda functions. (Written by ChatGPT)

C1. Basics of ChatGPT

C1.1. What is ChatGPT?

ChatGPT (short for "Chat Generative Pre-trained Transformer") is an
advanced AI language model developed by OpenAI. It is based on the
GPT architecture and is trained on a vast corpus of text data to
generate human-like responses. ChatGPT can understand context,
answer questions, and provide helpful information on a wide range of
topics, making it a valuable resource for learning programming
languages and other subjects.

C1.2. How does ChatGPT work?

ChatGPT works by analysing the input text and generating contextually
relevant responses based on its extensive training data. It uses a deep
learning architecture called transformers to process and generate text
in a parallel manner, enabling it to handle long-range dependencies
and produce coherent responses. The model is trained using a
technique called unsupervised learning, which allows it to generate text
based on patterns and relationships it has learned from the training
data.

C1.3. Benefits of using ChatGPT for learning programming languages

Some benefits of using ChatGPT for learning programming languages include:

- Quick access to explanations of concepts and syntax

- A wide range of code examples and demonstrations

- Debugging assistance and code review

- Recommendations for best practices, tips, and resources

- Exploration of advanced topics and techniques

C2. Learning Programming Languages with ChatGPT

C2.1. Asking for explanations of concepts and syntax

To learn concepts and syntax, simply ask ChatGPT questions or request explanations about specific programming concepts, keywords, or syntax. For example, "What is a class in Java?" or "How do loops work in Python?"

C2.2. Requesting code examples and demonstrations

Ask ChatGPT to provide code examples or demonstrate how to solve specific programming problems. For instance, "Show me an example of a for loop in C++" or "How to find the factorial of a number in JavaScript?"

C2.3. Debugging assistance and code review

If you have a piece of code that's not working correctly, you can share it with ChatGPT and ask for assistance in identifying and fixing any issues or improvements.

C2.4. Recommendations for best practices, tips, and resources

Ask ChatGPT for best practices, tips, and resources to learn a specific programming language or improve your programming skills. For example, "What are some best practices for writing clean Python code?" or "What resources can I use to learn Java?"

C2.5. Exploring advanced topics

As you become more proficient in a programming language, you can use ChatGPT to learn about more advanced topics like design patterns, data structures, algorithms, and language-specific libraries.

C3. Mastering Lambda Functions with ChatGPT

C3.1. Understanding the fundamentals of lambda functions

Ask ChatGPT to explain the basics of lambda functions, their usage, syntax, and characteristics in different programming languages.

C3.2. Comparing lambda functions in different programming languages

Request comparisons of lambda functions across various programming languages, highlighting similarities and differences in syntax and behaviour.

C3.3. Exploring advanced techniques and patterns for lambda functions

Ask ChatGPT about advanced techniques and patterns for working with lambda functions, such as currying, composition, and using lambda functions in conjunction with control structures.

C3.4. Requesting examples and use cases of lambda functions

Ask for examples and real-world use cases of lambda functions to understand their practical applications and advantages.

C3.5. Optimising lambda functions for performance and readability

Learn how to optimise lambda functions for better performance and readability, including best practices and common pitfalls to avoid.

C4. Complementary Learning Resources

C4.1. Books and online tutorials

Find books and online tutorials that cover the programming languages and concepts you're learning. These resources often provide in-depth explanations, examples, and exercises to help you master the material.

C4.2. Online courses and MOOCs

Take advantage of online courses and MOOCs (Massive Open Online Courses) from reputable platforms like Coursera, Udacity, and edX. These courses often cover a wide range of programming topics and are taught by experienced instructors.

C4.3. Coding exercises and practice platforms

Practice your programming skills using coding exercise websites and platforms like LeetCode, HackerRank, or Codecademy. These sites offer coding challenges and exercises to help you apply your knowledge and improve your skills.

C4.4. Engaging with the programming community

Join programming communities, forums, and social media groups to interact with other learners and experienced developers. This will provide you with valuable insights, advice, and opportunities to ask questions and share your knowledge.

C5. Tips for Effective Use of ChatGPT

C5.1. Asking clear and specific questions

To get the most out of ChatGPT, ask clear and specific questions. This will help the AI provide more accurate and relevant information.

C5.2. Verifying the accuracy of information provided by ChatGPT

While ChatGPT is a powerful tool, it's important to verify the accuracy of the information it provides. Cross-check answers and advice with other sources and resources to ensure correctness.

C5.3. Combining ChatGPT with other learning resources for a comprehensive learning experience

Use ChatGPT in conjunction with other learning resources like books, online courses, and tutorials to create a well-rounded learning experience.

C5.4. Regular practice and application of knowledge

Regularly apply the knowledge you gain from ChatGPT and other resources through practice exercises and real-world projects. This will help solidify your understanding and improve your programming skills.

C5.5. Setting goals and tracking progress

Set specific goals for your learning journey and track your progress over time. This will help you stay motivated and focused on improving your programming skills.

C5.6. Experimenting and learning from mistakes

Don't be afraid to experiment with different programming concepts and techniques. Learn from your mistakes and use ChatGPT to help you identify and understand any errors or misconceptions.

C5.7. Exploring various programming languages

As you become more comfortable with programming, consider exploring different languages and paradigms. This will broaden your perspective and help you become a more versatile programmer.

C5.8. Engaging in pair programming or code reviews

Collaborate with other learners or experienced developers through pair programming or code reviews. This will give you the opportunity to learn from others and receive valuable feedback on your code.

C5.9. Participating in programming challenges and hackathons

Join programming challenges, competitions, and hackathons to test your skills and learn from others in a competitive and collaborative environment.

C5.10. Staying up to date with industry trends and best practices

Keep up with the latest trends, best practices, and innovations in the programming world by reading blogs, following industry news, and attending conferences or workshops. This will ensure you stay current with new developments and techniques in the field.

By following these tips and leveraging ChatGPT as a learning resource, you'll be well on your way to mastering programming languages and concepts, including lambda functions. Remember to be patient, practice regularly, and maintain a curious mindset as you continue your learning journey.

Conclusion:

In this appendix, we have discussed how ChatGPT can be a powerful tool for learning programming languages and mastering lambda functions. By leveraging its capabilities to provide explanations, examples, and recommendations, you can enhance your understanding of various programming languages and concepts. However, it is crucial to remember that using ChatGPT effectively is just one part of your learning journey, and it should be combined with hands-on practice and other learning resources to ensure a comprehensive learning experience.

About the Author

Atheer Mahir is an accomplished AI prompt engineer and dedicated academic professional with a remarkable career spanning over 25 years. With expertise in academia, industry, and the business sectors, including the stock market, he brings a wealth of experience and knowledge to the table.

His educational background is rooted in Science, Computer Science, Mathematics, and advanced Physics, bolstering his proficiency in complex problem-solving. He has mastered AI-driven technologies and programming languages such as Mojo, Python, JavaScript, C#, and Swift for Apple app development. Holding both a Master's and Bachelor's degree in relevant fields, Atheer Mahir continuously incorporates the latest advancements into his work and stays abreast of emerging trends.

In addition to his technical prowess, Atheer Mahir has a passion for Photography, which reflects his creative approach to problem-solving and his ability to visualise complex concepts.

Atheer Mahir primarily focuses on Python (or Mojo for the future) and AI, constantly honing his AI engineering skills with the goal of creating innovative and efficient applications for the future. His expertise in JavaScript, C#, and Swift enables him to develop versatile solutions across various platforms, with a special emphasis on Apple app development.

He is an enthusiastic learner and actively engages with online platforms such as LinkedIn Learning, EDX.org, and Coursera, ensuring he stays at the forefront of his field. As an AI prompt engineer, he is committed to empowering others with the knowledge and resources necessary to excel and contribute to the advancement of technology in diverse sectors, particularly in Computer Science, Mathematics, and advanced Physics. His passion for education, coupled with his extensive experience, technical expertise, and creative skills, makes him a valuable asset in any academic, research, or industrial setting.

With a proven track record and a relentless drive for innovation, Atheer Mahir is poised to make significant contributions to the field and leave an indelible mark on the intersection of AI and technology. [For latest articles and published books: https://bit.ly/ldn1]

bit.ly/kdpDesigns

Creative Designs By ADMSLC